MERCHANDISING
by DESIGN

MERCHANDISING by DESIGN

Developing Effective Menus & Wine Lists

LEONARD F. FELLMAN

Lebhar-Friedman Books
Chain Store Age Publishing Corp.
A Subsidiary of Lebhar-Friedman Inc.
New York

Copyright © 1981, Chain Store Publishing Corp., 425 Park Avenue, New York, N.Y. 10022.

Printed in the United States of America

Book Design: Harriet Hoffman

Library of Congress Cataloging in Publication Data:
Fellman, Leonard F., 1922-
  Merchandising by design

  1. Menus. 2. Wine lists. 3. Wine and
wine making. I. Title.
TX911.3.M45F44   642'.5'0688   81-18117
ISBN: 0-86730-237-2   AACR2

5   4   3   2   1

CONTENTS

Part I Menus

Part II Wine Lists

Appendix

ILLUSTRATIONS

PART I

MENUS

1

YOUR MENU AND
YOUR ESTABLISHMENT

There are two points of view regarding the preparation and planning of a menu. One follows the literal French translation of the word menu: "a small detailed list of the foods available to patrons." The second sees the menu as an imaginative chart which invites the reader into a new world of tastes, aromas, after-tastes, flavorings, and nuances that excite the palate and the brain.

Practical limitations and considerations surround all menus and wine lists, from the moment of design until the time they reach the guest. But there is no limit to the imaginative factor. Coffee shop, fast food operation, and gourmet white cloth restaurant all have one aim in their menus: to tell the diner what they offer, at what price, in the most forceful manner.

Yesterday, the restaurateur knew each guest, the guest's family, problems, and business. He personally took the menu to the table, and his personality was projected with the menu. Today, that restaurateur has disappeared; operations are larger and more impersonal. Suddenly the menu takes on a greater importance as the personal representative of the management. Food servers and maître d's may change, but the menu, through the image it projects continues as the link between customer and restaurant. The menu therefore warrants complete attention. It should be thought out in depth in every aspect—color, size, design, and handling. The menu should reflect your personality or the image which you are attempting to create; it should be yours, and yours alone. The job of planning, producing, and creating a menu is time consuming. However, the time and effort are rewarded in the end.

One gourmet restaurant in Paris put a lot of creative planning into their menu. The Captain introduced himself and suddenly there appeared, in costume, a young lady who, the Captain explained, was "La Belle Menu." We were each handed what appeared to be a children's storybook. The cover was a farmyard scene. Each page was folio size. The first right-hand page was an illustration of an orange duck outlined in black. Across the bottom was a reproduction of Napoleon's signature. There was no restaurant name or other descriptive copy. The following left page told the story of Napoleon's visit to the restaurant. The facing right page was a full recipe and description of the various ways in which their duck was prepared. Each page carried a single illustration—a chicken, a cow, etc. The vegetable section was a colorful montage of vegetables over a garden scene—the quickest representation ever of the statement "our vegetables are garden fresh."

Absorbed in the presentation, we almost overlooked "La Belle Menu" who was standing next to a blackboard with the meal of the day pictured in chalk.

One more touch: at the conclusion of the meal we were presented with another storybook. However, in place of the menu there was an actual children's story. I asked the proprietor for an explanation of the thinking behind the menu. The Gallic answer was to the point. "The world of good food knows our name; to further the guest's enjoyment we wished him or her to completely relax. What better way than a simple storybook approach to the fine things of nature? Most fine restaurants have the same menu. Our cuisine is unique and high quality, and the image we wanted the customer to retain was one of elegant simplicity."

In any city, if you were to visit the most elegant restaurants, you would find all their menus looking very much the same—closely resembling a bank statement. The owner probably spends more time on one entrée in the kitchen than his total time in developing the menu "look." If the management of a superior restaurant will spend endless time searching for a chef, then why not take the time to develop a menu that impresses the guest, as much as the quality of the fine food that brought him there originally.

On the outskirts of Des Moines, Iowa, there is a diner where the menu cover illustrates license plates from every state. The back cover has the logos of the trucks and truck lines that use the diner. On the center spread, ghosted in the background behind the menu type, is a drawing of the principal highways that cross the state. A metal spinner is grommetted onto the menu in the lower right-hand corner. Customers receive colored semi trailers, with the rules of the game, and are encouraged to take the menu as a souvenir. An unmistakable image is projected in the names of the entrées: the Gear Box Burger, Transmission Special breakfast, Long Haul take-out chicken dinner. An illustration accompanies each one. Because most Americans believe that truck stops serve good food at fair prices, this diner has worked at emphasizing that image to establish this eating place as belonging to the truckers' world.

Yellowstone National Park has much to offer visitors. Raft trips, tours, and other activities are available. The park is full of outdoor adventure, but how to get the many-sided story of different park activities to the restaurant guest in the park? The decision was reached to use the menu as a vehicle of communication at a time when the guest is at leisure. Each hotel in the park has its own menu, but basically they are all the same. As each mealtime called for its own menu, the story was broken down: one menu has a complete map of the park on the back cover, locating campsites and points of interest. (See Fig. 1) Other back covers are used to list activities. The colors of the stock follow through on the outdoors theme. These were carefully selected in woodland hues; matching inks add to the atmosphere. All menu items carry names associated with the park—Powder Horn Potluck, The Glacier, etc. The departing visitor who has dined at the various restaurants is therefore exposed repeatedly to park elements, and if interested can take the complete menu collection as a unique remembrance.

Placing the guest in a position where he or she becomes part of

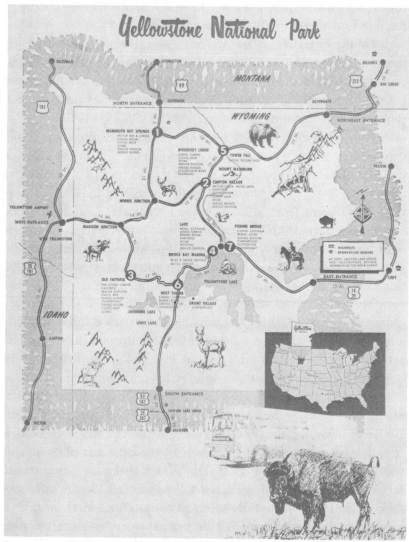

Fig. 1 One coffeeshop in Yellowstone National Park has a map of the park on the back cover of the menu.

the scene increases the importance of his or her role. The menu must never be isolated—it is necessary that it be part of the total structuring of the establishment.

Every menu must fit with the psychology of the restaurant. A fast food restaurant must carry a cover that conveys the sense of immediate service (The Road Runner). Entrées must be in large type, numbered for quick ordering with boldface prices. Dishes must be described in the simplest terms. Illustrations save time and assist selection. Expediting the ordering process involves the guest in the sense of convenience and restaurant competence, an understanding that the establishment respects his or her time.

THE MENU—A CUSTOMER'S EYE VIEW

The menu is the communications link between your customer, yourself, and your kitchen. The size, color, and wording should produce a menu that is informative, complete, and easily read. At the same time, it should be so notably constructed as to alert the senses, stimulate the reader, and provide a full measure of confidence.

There should be no room for error or misunderstanding. The kitchen should deliver what is stated on the menu. Attractive enough to be remembered, the menu should not so overwhelm the customer that the presentation of the actual food is out of proportion to what he or she has anticipated. The menu must be in keeping with the positioning and market of the establishment. It must be comfortably sized in proportion to the table, its coloration in keeping with the decor. Ease of handling simplifies the presentation by staff and handling by customer. Proper sizing avoids knocked-over table settings and menus that interfere with other table guests.

It should be informative, responding to what the diner wants to know about where he or she is dining. It should tie in with the image of the restaurant. A truck driver at a truck stop would hardly appreciate a hand-lettered manuscript on parchment.

A clearly marked "House Specialties" section gives the newcomer an insight or hint on ordering. Educational courtesy can stir the sense as well: "Idaho Mountain Trout" rather than "trout." "Goulash Magyar" is more gracious than "Hungarian Goulash." "Sourdough Bread" does not provide the message that "Sourdough Bread in the San Francisco tradition" gets across. "Chicken Kiev" sounds marvelous—but—your customer may ask "What is Chicken Kiev?" The cohesive menu takes nothing for granted. Not every customer is a world-traveled gourmet. That customer has intelligence. Information is not insulting; it avoids areas of complaint and misunderstanding.

A restaurant does not have to be a five-star applicant to be proud of its kitchen and its food. The consummate menu brings together the facts, arranging the food in a sequence that enables the guest to select without strain, thereby allowing him or her to actually participate in the putting together of the meal.

It is the excitement and uniqueness of the presentation in the menu that will make a potential diner state, "They've got a fantastic selection." The contents may be similar to that of other menus, the prices alike, but the manner in which the menu items are set forth makes the difference. A hamburger that is a "Hot and juicy hamburger" must be better than a "Hamburger."

The brain creates images from words: "corn-fed beef," "dairy-fresh eggs," "homemade soup"—what pictures rush to the mind? Why confuse the guest with foreign words and phrases that literally force him or her to ask or, avid to avoid embarrassment, order another dish? If your clientele will enjoy foreign cooking terms such as "bouquetierre," "flambé," "au jus" and this will enhance your image, fine. But I recall an extensive lecture presentation by a chef who used so many of these phrases the audience was lost looking for an interpreter. If your steaks are aged, if they are from prize-winning cattle, you owe this information to your diner. A famed Atlanta restaurant captions a huge segment of their menu "All Hail the Georgia Peach. There simply is nothing as great as a Georgia Peach—and our Peaches must wear a Blue Ribbon." A list is provided to the customer of over fifty ways he or she will enjoy the pleasures of "Our Georgia Peaches."

I always enjoy the French restaurant in New York with a menu entirely in the French translated underneath into the various slangs

Fig. 2 Menu cover, the Pacific Hotel, St. Joseph Mo. Photo courtesy of Bohn-Bettoni Collection, University of Nevada, Las Vegas Library.

and idioms of different sections of the U.S. Or the concoction that carries the name of a theatrical or athletic personality.

Then there is the Dallas restaurant that must have searched endlessly for the right saying or proverb to apply to each specific dish. Perhaps this type of effort put into developing a restaurant's personality through its menus is what creates a Sardi's, Brown Derby, or Ruby Foo.

Certainly the chef, cooking, and service are a substantial part of the differences among restaurants, but the fact is that charm and the character are an achievement. Your zest for success must be matched by your pride and thoughtfulness in letting your customers know fully what you offer.

There is a fast-growing chain of better Italian restaurants that somehow discovered that people enjoy watching a spaghetti-making machine. Impossible? Never. At the window and from within the restaurant, they watch as eagerly as if the greatest scientific event of the century were taking place. Management goes further and has old illustrations of spaghetti as it was made centuries ago. The menu describes and illustrates the various types of pasta and gives recipes for sauces. Everyone knows how spaghetti is made, or do they?

Stop at the Lobster Pot at Logan Airport in Boston and watch an endless line of busy executives attentive to the slightest move that the lobsters make. One impressive fish restaurant has a menu clip-on headed "Today's Fish Story." It tells the name of the vessel that the day's catch came from and the name of its captain, and lists the fish that were caught and are being served.

What are you doing that is provocative, that makes a customer return to find out what you have to say that will take him or her away from the ordinary? The personalities of the restaurant may be your key. I am reminded of the menu of Shoyers of Philadelphia, which talked of their original establishment, their servers, and their owners. Or perhaps the chef will be a personality with whom the guest can identify.

A clever owner keeps a pad for doodlers—"Don't scribble, help us write our menu." The customer is invited to describe favorite dishes served by the restaurant. The menu is reprinted every three months, and if the guest's description is used as written, his or her name appears, and he or she is sent a bottle of champagne.

The words used to describe your foods need not be lengthy. The menu becomes a communication link if the words fit in with the atmosphere and terminology your guests expect. Your menu is more than ink and paper, leather and gold, it is the magic carpet of your restaurant. A revolution in menu presentation is taking place. The day of the lavish leather or plastic cover into which the menu is inserted is disappearing. The gold tassel no longer hangs down. The menu cover is part of the overall presentation. It fits the restaurant's decor, and its ingenuity and creative concept sell the menu contents. The concept used on the cover is almost always followed through in the interior of the menu.

THE MENU AND THE STAFF

Too many managers rush the menu from the printer to the customer. The first look the server gets is when he or she presents it to the customer. To fully merchandise the creative menu, total involvement all the way through is needed.

A staff meeting should be arranged to merchandise a menu. The chef should explain the dishes, the bar manager should review the wines and spirits, management should explain the philosophy followed in planning the menu. An item-by-item review should follow, with certain dishes selected for tasting. If any foreign phrases are used these should be explained.

Merchandising the menu relies almost completely on the staff. The greater their knowledge, the more credible their recommendations to customers. The well thought out and planned menu combined with a well trained and organized staff will help create a fine restaurant. Success in the food service industry proves itself with guests who return and a clientele that grows.

When food servers have a menu to present that is comprehensive, time saving, and attractive, they will have increased confidence in their presentation.

The subliminal reaction of the customer to a menu that is above average in concept, better thought out, and more attractively cre-

ated is that the establishment is concerned about the customer.
Menus and wine lists cannot be created for the ego and desire of the
management; they must perform a service for all involved.

The hard question therefore is whether or not the work of the
menu and wine list is clearly understood in all its functions. When it
is worked out, clarified, and properly presented, it becomes, next to
the quality of the cookery, the most important element of the
establishment.

1. It must be complete. A customer should be able to order
   without needing to ask questions.
2. It must be legible. There should be no strain on the
   reader.
3. The colors should be coordinated with the decor, so that
   when placed on the table, it will clearly belong there.
4. It should be the proper size in proportion to total room
   and table.
5. Durability and cleanliness are important. Secure a sample of the stock and fold and refold to test how that paper
   will stand up.
6. Does the design reflect the image you are building?
7. Are you proud of this document, the soul of your establishment?

HISTORICAL BACKGROUND

In France in about 1765, Pierre Boulanger placed a poster
announcing the special of the day on his restaurant door. Soon this
pattern caught on and the name of the chef was added, and on
special occasions there were festoons and decorations. Up to this
date the menu served a practical function. It was the coordinating
communiqué between the kitchen, the master, the maître d', and
the staff of servers.

To gain extra gratuities, the maître d' would write the menu on
strips of cloth and the guest would be presented with the menu. He
might consult his list secretly under the tablecloth. This was a most

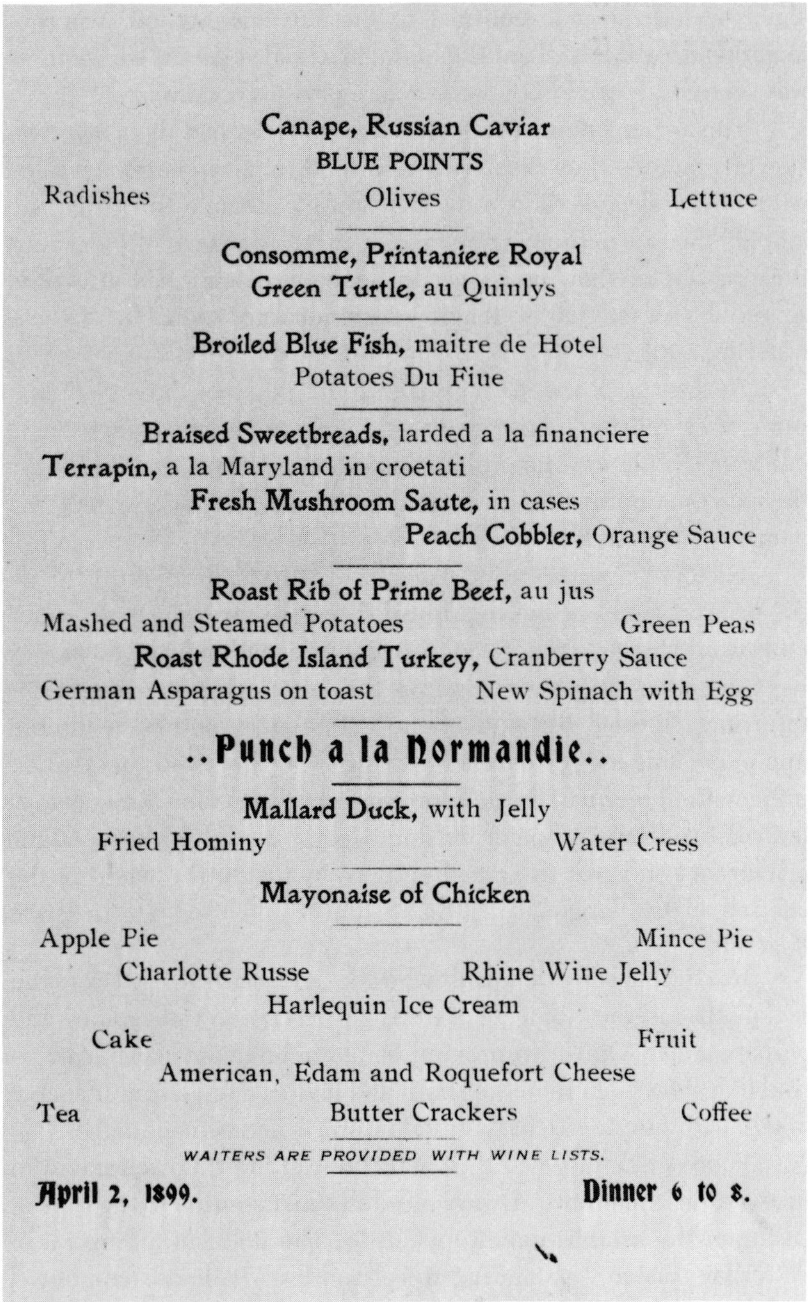

Canape, Russian Caviar
BLUE POINTS

Radishes   Olives   Lettuce

Consomme, Printaniere Royal
Green Turtle, au Quinlys

Broiled Blue Fish, maitre de Hotel
Potatoes Du Fiue

Braised Sweetbreads, larded a la financiere
Terrapin, a la Maryland in croetati
Fresh Mushroom Saute, in cases
Peach Cobbler, Orange Sauce

Roast Rib of Prime Beef, au jus
Mashed and Steamed Potatoes   Green Peas
Roast Rhode Island Turkey, Cranberry Sauce
German Asparagus on toast   New Spinach with Egg

..Punch a la Normandie..

Mallard Duck, with Jelly
Fried Hominy   Water Cress

Mayonaise of Chicken

Apple Pie   Mince Pie
Charlotte Russe   Rhine Wine Jelly
Harlequin Ice Cream
Cake   Fruit
American, Edam and Roquefort Cheese
Tea   Butter Crackers   Coffee

WAITERS ARE PROVIDED WITH WINE LISTS.

April 2, 1899.   Dinner 6 to 8.

Fig. 3 Antique menu. Photo courtesy of Bohn-Bettoni Collection, University of Nevada, Las Vegas Library.

sophisticated move in contrast to the Russian method, where a major domo would yell out the menu in a loud voice. As each course was served, he would bellow its name plus his comments.

The ancient Roman trattorias and tavernas had their own version of a menu—they displayed their foods in glass amphoras filled with water, alcohol, and salt. This would enhance the color and amplify the size of the portion. Today, in many areas of the Far East the practice of showing dishes is done by placing well-executed reproductions on view, so that the customer knows what he or she is ordering.

As the use of menus moved into the nineteenth century, the work of established artists such as Toulouse Lautrec was used to decorate the menu. The problem was that guests preferred to study their own menu instead of observing the one original carried by a member of the staff.

History keeps repeating itself. At the turn of the century, when the printed menu began to appear, the more sophisticated restaurants would list the courses on the right side, and indicate the wines recommended for each course on the left. Today that practice is returning. Toward the end of the eighteenth century, a limited number of inns and restaurants catering to the moneyed guest would prepare their menu in French and English, supporting their claim of international or European cuisine. Today, a multitude of ethnic restaurants enhance their authenticity by giving the name of the offering in the language of their country and then a translation beneath.

It is the conscientious host who goes a step further and cites the region that is the home of the dish, then gives the recipe, and perhaps a map. One entrepreneur has a star on the map of his native land that shows where he was born and invites guests from that area to talk with him to discuss mutual interests and acquaintances.

Food is a fantasy world, so why not capture this excitement in the words of the menu? Always give full consideration to the type of customer the establishment appeals to. The Pullman dining car of yesterday was an outstanding travel venture. Railroads competed with each other to furnish travelers with the finest array of local foods, and their menus were highly innovative. It was here that the first menu with calorie counts appeared. Presentations were in full color and were used to depict historic events of the land that the train rolled through. Dishes were described in detail. The wild turkey came from the forests at Strobridge, the steaks from the Great Plains of the Dakotas. One super deluxe diner offered beef Wellington—with a magnificent portrait of the English hero and the story of the dish's creation.

This same possibility of using memorabilia and historical and geographical details to entice the diner is more available today than ever before, yet few take advantage of surrounding their offerings with romance.

2

MENU DESIGN

The menu is like the creation of a musical piece; it must all come together as a complete unit. This applies to every menu for every food service operation, be it a gourmet restaurant or a coffee bar. Once the theme is established, every aspect comes into place.

The art of menu preparation is an important one in establishing the significance and position of the dining establishment.

USING PROFESSIONALS

Many professionals, such as printers, advertising agencies and art services specialize in producing menus. Stock menu houses will set covers and inserts and can personalize a menu by imprinting your logo on it. Most of these houses maintain a library of illustrations, proverbs, and statements having to do with food. This is one of the least expensive methods of producing a menu. An alert restaurant owner can work with the available material and create an individualized menu. Although costs are standard, it is best to get estimates and insist on seeing a finished proof prior to printing.

Artwork is costly. Every segment of the process—art, layout,

Fig. 4 Menu cover, Hotel Normandie, Chicago. Photo courtesy of Bohn-Bettoni Collection, University of Nevada, Las Vegas Library.

typography, can be expensive. Each time a change is made your costs increase. While changes are possible at all stages of production, they will consume time and money. It is wise to know precisely what you want done before going to a printer. Having actual samples that illustrate specifics will make economies possible.

Prepare a file that contains as much material as possible for the artist and writer. Jot down your thoughts on color and design as well as any significant ideas that you think will add greater individuality. Compile your own menu collection. Include samples of illustrations and typography that reflect your taste. Don't just turn your menu and list over to a professional. Without your guiding hand you may get back a competent but highly impersonal layout.

PROJECTING YOUR IMAGE

The professional menu printer and designer are only as capable as the information furnished by you. They must be given direction. Lack of direction in menu planning may be as harmful as a lack of direction in the kitchen.

What message does the restaurant wish to communicate to its customers? Have the policy and contents of the menu been completely discussed with the chef, owners, ad agency?

The end result should be a menu that brings together all the ideas into a unified image. Some of the finest ideas are introduced by customers and staff. But the bringing together of the message is the job of the professional. There are endless types of stock (paper) and inks; the blending together with the decor of the restaurant is a necessity.

A new restaurant opening in Atlantic City had selected an unusual imported wallpaper on their walls. To reinforce the customers' impression of the restaurant, the owner used the wallpaper as the menu cover.

The bar of a certain New York restaurant is historically famous. Management had color photos of the bar reproduced on its menu, which was die-cut in the shape of the bar. The details of the old spitoon, bartenders with mustaches, drinks on the bar, old prices are all there. As the menu unfolds to the length of the bar so does its story. The list is a collector's find. What makes it truly different is that the creator searched through catalogs of printing papers and finally unearthed paper with a wood-type texture in a walnut finish. The menu printer can save you hours once given the information as to the "look" that will suit your needs. If you frequent restaurants on Fifty-second Street in New York, in the Near North side of Chicago, or in Beverly Hills, the sameness of the menu papers and the typefaces will be disappointing. One would think that with their creative staffs and substantial budgets these eating places would have mindboggling menus. Not so. It is the smaller, more individualized owner whose ingenuity must work where one sees gratifying results. Ideas in menu design come from everywhere. The more papers and treatments that are presented the more options you have in choosing your image.

A fine restaurant in Chicago which had a traditional menu for years decided to take an aggressive stand and develop a menu to meet its new standards.

A printer presented a sample of a parchment paper which carried an imitation seal. The restaurant owners were taken by the regal look of the signet and fine paper. Working with a staff artist they developed a comprehensive plan. The list was reproduced in solid black ink from a hand-lettered original, with illuminated headings drawn in the manner of the manuscripts produced by monks. The initial letter was heavily ornate. Upon conclusion of the meal the guest was presented with a manuscript attesting to his having dined, to which was affixed a reproduction of a seal. The search that began for a paper wound up with a total look with a strong impact.

The modern miracle of protective finishes may produce as much harm as good; impartial reactions are a necessity in considering them. There are two basic types of protective finishes against dirt, fingerprints, spillage, etc. The most effective is lamination. This is done by enclosing the menu within a heat-sealed laminant. The surface is completely washable, the menu completely sealed. This type of protective coating is ideally suited to fast food, air terminal, or coffee shop operations where high traffic and heavy turnover are a hazard that can turn a well designed menu into a mess

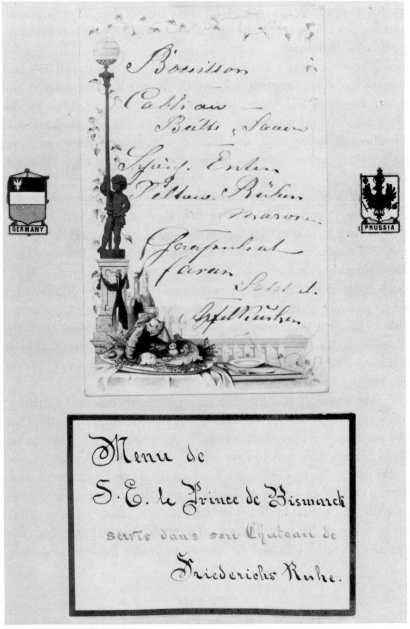

Fig. 5 Antique menu. Photo courtesy of Bohn-Bettoni Collection, University of Nevada, Las Vegas Library.

in minutes. As most of the menus of these operations use color photos, the lamination adds to the vivid presentation. Over a period of time, the savings through lamination as against constant replacement are substantial.

The second type of finish is a chemical coating sprayed over the menu while it is being printed. Not as effective as lamination, it has positive assets which lamination lacks, such as retaining the feel to the hand of the texture of the stock. The subtleties in reproduction of the illustrations are maintained for a quality image. More and more airlines have returned to the unlaminated menu for a soft, classic art look.

Menus made entirely of plastic are mainly used by major chain operations. I am of the opinion that their artificial look is sales-destructive; it makes the patron conscious of being in a chain operation and may also make him or her wonder whether the meals are also impersonal and chemical. False economy will destroy a hard-built image. A luxury gourmet restaurant in a major hotel laminated its menus. Customers repeatedly commented on the "coffee shop" look. The servers refused to present the menu, stating that the glossy look did not reflect the expensive pricing and fine quality of the food. The magnificence of the menu art was completely lost in the presentation.

The typical chain operation menu is a lesson in lack of initiative. When menus from different chains are placed alongside each other the sameness is apparent: a large color photo, a few impersonal descriptive words, and you are served. While the selling technique could remain as is, certainly a few line illustrations, different foldings, a specific character of the text could all be pieced together to establish the positive identity of the restaurant. Staggering amounts go into research, advertising, and marketing groups, but the menu—the crux of the selling—seems to receive the least attention.

COLOR

Menu art reflects the image of the times. The importance of the menu became noticeable in France at the beginning of the nineteenth century. With the signing of the Peace of Amiens in 1803, restaurants developed covers that related to Napoleon and the era of peace and prosperity. Menu art included maps showing historic sights, and illustration of political partisanships. Famed artists were hired to paint important events for the menu cover. Portraits of personalities were extremely popular, as were magnificent illustrations having to do with the specialities of the restaurant.

Most covers were in full color, many carried embossing and engraving. An 1884 dinner for the Fish Supply Committee, given in the London Guildhall, had a full color underwater scene depicting sea life in its natural environment. A menu of a New York restaurant called Renowned Rectors, of Diamond Jim Brady and Lillian Russell fame, illustrated angels carrying wine and food, while in the center a beautiful figure offered a champagne toast. The historic menu of nineteenth-century Paris's Le Pavillion was created by artist Bernard Lamotte, and in Chicago the Pump Room's menu included engravings of the turbaned waiters who specialized in the serving of flaming dishes.

Good art is timeless. To use color effectively it must not clash with the table setting nor with the room decor. It should be colorful without being glaring. Color in menus must be cautiously planned, observed, and tested prior to actual use.

An outdoor restaurant at Marina Del Rey, California, prints its menus on brown kraft paper. The menu performs double duty for the restaurant and the takeout department. The menu is printed in deep brown, showing local sites and tides. A map illustrates shoals, tides, and reefs as well as channels.

An air force base in Nevada used the cover of *Time* and inserted in-flight photos of three planes in use at the air base. (See Fig. 6) The red color of the cover matched the tablecloth, and was carried out in the names of entrees.

In Washington, D.C., a military base reproduced a commemorative plate with reproductions of military heroes on its menu cover. The theme colors were blue and white, matching the drapery and wallpaper.

Color creates atmosphere, and where possible should be employed in creating a theme. The effect of color plus texture can give you the perfect combination. A major hotel, in opening a new branch in Portland, Oregon, took advantage of being in the "Rose

Fig. 6 Menu cover, Nellis Officer's Club.

City." Using a flocked burgundy paper as a cover for both their wine list and menu, then imprinting the burgundy with gold, they gained immediate local approval.

A seafood restaurant in San Francisco took wine corks, drilled a hole down their centers, sliced them, and threaded twine across the hollow slices. These rows of corks were mounted on a blue foil background. In one brief moment the customer absorbs the seafood background. The menu is printed in tones of blue ink with a cut-off cork mounted atop the wine list. The texture of the cork, the color of the sea, came together in a romantic nautical image.

A brilliant color and texture concept was used by a coffee house in the Greenwich Village area of New York City. The owner purchased the same type of burlap bags that coffee beans are shipped in. He mountd them on cardboard covers, and stenciled in the names of the exotic coffees served. The "ears" of the bag were added and twisted into position with twine, beans were glued onto the burlap—a total story.

A deli in Boston printed its menu as a giant punch ticket. Instead of the prices, there were illustrations of the sandwiches, platters, and drinks. Prices are given below the illustrations. The entire ticket was arranged similarly to the fairway game where the participant swings a hammer, sending up a weight to ring the bell along a board with markings depicting his strength. The top deli item was a Macho Macho Club sandwich at high cost. This was their best seller.

There is no rule that menu prices must be in black, yet this morbid color appears everywhere. The current trend of color usage away from the traditional black on color or white, can upgrade and underline the points of interest. Headings are now in a color that matches the basic decor. This simple expedient breaks formality. By employing the "ghosting" or screened color technique of using a tone or tint of the color in a background and the full-strength solid color elsewhere, a two-color effect is created.

A military base in Oklahoma used a collection of old artillery scenes on its menu. Pricing and information were printed in deep rust brown and a tone of this color was used in the "ghosted" illustrations. The menus became collectors' memorabilia.

The ethnic restaurant serving national specialties that wants to achieve a specific color approach based on national colors can bounce colors, by alternating them in captions.

In Reno, Nevada, one diner places an illustration of the platter in a circle, with the name of the dish surrounding the plate like the lettering on a silver dollar. The complete menu illustration is done in silver and black. The front cover is dollar green, designed to look like a bank passbook.

An inexpensive means of gaining a multicolor look is to print the cover in one color and then use an entirely different color on the inside. I was recently shown a menu done for an airport in New England. The front cover was executed in solid green, and the lettering in white in the color of the paper. Within the menu, the reverse had been done—inside was solid white with printing in deep green. Thus, the operation paid for a one-color printing and received a two-color effect. In addition, many cover papers are duo-colored, giving the impression of multiple color without the cost. Color in menu design must never be forced; it must be chosen with justifiable reason and with balance in mind.

DESIGN

There is a theory that a successful menu should have fifty percent white space, with art and copy occupying the balance of the area. The art and layout determine the atmosphere the menu conveys. It is a fact of life that budgets place a hold on expenditures, but this in no way should stand in the way of a successful, creative menu.

The first step is to prepare the menu listing, determining the amount of space it will take up. This is the time to also consider the length of the wine list. If it is lengthy, it calls for a separate brochure, though this does not preclude listing a recommended wine under each entree or alongside the servings.

Once all segments of the menu list are laid out, the space devoted to additional factors such as the history of the establishment, proverbs, and accessory information must be planned so that the full extent of the space needed is known.

Type is an important consideration when planning the overall look of the menu. There are thousands of typefaces. Readability and theme play their part in selection. Choosing the elegance of an engraver's script compared with the richness of a Caslon, the humor of Cartoon, or the many early American and western faces plays a part in the final integration of art and copy. The final decision rests on the response you want from customers. Your local printer has a catalogue of typefaces to look at when deciding on type.

Your staff's and diners' reaction to your menu may not be obvious on the surface, but keep it in mind when you plan. The use of foreign phrases, for example, must either be accompanied by an order number of an English translation; neither staff nor diner enjoys appearing unlearned.

Borders are effective. One well-known German restaurant borders its menu with pictures of costumes of various districts. Then, next to each entrée is a costume illustration from the region where the dish was created.

Years ago I was given a full color menu done for Stouffer's, which was extremely well done. Every page had a large illustration of a vegetable, and the inside border picked up the exterior illustrations for a unified look. A border of food and wine can prove highly effective: One sophisticated menu carries a small illustration in the bottom corner of a wine wagon collecting grapes.

A Las Vegas menu showed different winning symbols alongside all their entrées, which were named accordingly: the High Roller, the Pit Boss, etc.

Die cutting, while expensive, will add much to a menu. A western diner die cut a stagecoach into its cover. Inside, the listing was in the shape of a "Wanted" poster, entrées were symbolized by a marshal's badge, handcuffs, etc. A fast food menu cover showed two construction workers eating their lunch atop a girder far above the street. "We deliver anywhere" read the caption.

COST CONTROL IN REPRODUCTION

In planning, it is vital to bear in mind that art is expensive. Obviously, quantity makes the difference in bringing down costs. Therefore, before art is finalized, printing costs must be established.

One economy step is to print only as many menus as are needed immediately with prices and leave the balance blank. A further step for protection in the event of menu changes is to simply print covers, and imprint as needed.

Preparing full-color art and later discovering that the reproduction expense is prohibitive can be disastrous. Planning ahead to find the most cost-effective method of reproduction will help. More restaurants are utilizing the silk-screen process to achieve unusual effects, especially in short runs. This process is applicable to fabric, wood, foil, or paper. It can produce raised flock and glittered effect and has a vibrancy of color. It may be protectively lacquered. The one cautionary note in using silk screen is that type must be sufficiently large to be read in the restaurant's lighting.

The fact is that the most elegant of menus are the simplest. One of the great five-star restaurants uses on its cover a simple one-color art deco illustration on a flocked gray background. It is not always the full-color treatment that creates the maximum effect. The menu cover of an Italian restaurant in Los Angeles carries a reproduction of a daguerreotype of the owners' parents on arrival to this country. One of my favorite menu illustrations has always been a drawing of pots and pans hanging from the wall, with a chef's hat in the foreground. Another favorite is a simple illustration done in pen and ink of a fruit knife in an orange with a champagne cork to the side.

There are stock photo services that will inexpensively furnish photos for reproduction for almost any situation. The seafood house that desires a photo of a fisherman or trawler, the steak house that seeks a grazing scene may find such a service quick and economical.

Some restaurants are so proud of their decor that their cover is the original architect's or interior designer's sketch.

IMPACT OF THE WELL-DESIGNED MENU

The remarkable part of menus that are strong image- and business-builders is that they originate from research that is obvious, freely available, and far less costly than purchased art. To adapt this material the creator must think out how he or she desires to position the business, the most fundamental manner to tell the story quickly and thoroughly, what he or she offers that makes the establishment unique, and how to design a cover so creative that when lying flat it is a standard-bearer for what is to follow.

Lack of initiative is the failure of most menus. At a recent state restaurant convention I was approached by a member and his daughter. They owned a restaurant in a large industrial town that was growing and prospering. The food service business there was dominated by two major hotel chains along with chain operations. The father and daughter claimed they could afford to produce a menu and wine list that would take on the competition. They showed me their menu; the cover was a typical stock product, but when the menu was opened the dishes themselves were fascinating. They were local specialties prepared from authentic recipes of the region. The restaurant was being operated by the second generation of the family that had founded it. They served a family, moderate income clientele. Asked whether any particular incident had occurred around the time the restaurant opened that would quickly establish how long they had been in existence, the owners answered that the restaurant opened the day Charles Lindbergh landed in Paris.

Pointing to this historic event that would mark the length of time in operation, I suggested they contact the local papers for copies of that day's edition. Further, they could approach the public relations departments of local industries for photos of the plants as they were then as well as for more recent photos. Those businesses which arrived in town recently might have illustrations of their products as they were made at that time.

I suggested that the menu be converted to a miniature tabloid, printed on newspaper stock, with the original of each menu item fully explained. They could include information about the families who had created the recipes, while emphasizing that they were the sole restaurant offering these specialties. Other articles could tie together the history of the restaurant's founders with the city, and space could be given to local current events. Customers would be encouraged to take copies with them.

There was no reason to spend on art and preparation. Copy could be written by the family, and a local printer could produce the paper at very little expense.

This meeting occurred in May, 1979. Christmas of that year I

THE BACK FORTY HARD TIMES

SAN FRANCISCO BAY AREA AND LAS VEGAS

THE BACK FORTY HARD TIMES

The *Back Forty Hard Times* is a non-profit, rarely published publication having significant interest only to rustlers, the overweight and non-literary connoisseurs offering no significant news value to the American literate populace.

ITCHIN' N' SCRATCHIN'

Warning — Quarratine: Texas Tic Fever hit south Texas to the Pecos Valley. A special quarratine was placed by Doctor Almos Bensure on the entire Area of Pecan Valley, just north of Blue Ridge. Doc Bensure was sure he could stop the Tic Fever with special medication and injections given to the precautioned area. So far, seventy lives have been lost in Pecan Valley and the thicket range. Doctor Henry Sawsure, cousin to Doc Bensure, was the county agent in charge of all burials. Doctors Bensure, Sawsure felt the fever would be under control by winter. Doctor Sawsure made sure Bensure was sure to check the afflicted members' families were quarantined as well. Both doctors felt the epidemic would probably take the lives of only twenty or thirty more ticks stricken with the fever.

The Health Jolting Chair

Back Forty Goes Way Back

The term "Back Forty" dates back to the days of the government land grants during the seventeen and eighteen hundreds. Back Forty also relates to terminology used in the Northwestern logging camps.

During the time in American History when immigrants from the Eastern United States and Foreign countries were migrating out west, the U.S. government opened new lands for homestead. These grants consisted of 640 acres, each divided into four sections of 160 acres to each section. A quarter section was forty acres. A landowner referred to the forty acres farthest from his dwelling as the "Back Forty." Hence the term "Back Forty," or, in other words, the portion of land way out back. Familiar cousins to the term "Back Forty" are the North Forty and South Forty as well as ole East and West Forty.

According to other western or northwestern lore, the term "Back Forty" is used in logging camps. Loggers apply "Back Forty" to any distant place, the back end of a logging operation and beyond. Lastly, it is a term meaning the ideal logging location one never finds. Similar to the land grants in the west, were logging grants in similar proportions given to the logging companies near the same period of time.

Due to no recorded date, person, or area of the United States claiming the origin of the term "Back Forty", we must presume that it came about because, ONE, it was a fur piece away from where the person was that thought of "Back Forty". TWO, He only knew how to count to forty as did his friends who passed the term along.

CATCHED TETCHED FETCHED

Wanted: Dude Ranch needs cowboy between the ages of 75 and 95 docile toward the gentler sex. Must be strong enough to turn away familiar hostile intentions from older feminine guests without total rejection. Knowledge of horses and ranch work not a necessity.

For Sale: Elmer Coogin's branch water, especially cured from range dew left on elm branches for 6 days. This water is not a cure-all for animals, but is a tremendous ointment for human sickness, sores, aches and pains. One in a hundred bottles contains an added ingredient of formaldehyde for those who have insomnia. Price: 1 quart — 5¢, 1 gallon — 15 ¢, cork no extra charge.

For Hire: One Indian maiden, will work for room and board and a small consideration (two good ponies and six moons supply of fire water) for father. She excellent cook, know'em horses, can pull'em plow, chop'em wood and clean'em and keep'em wig-wam' warm' til frost on mountain fall to valley and make'm heep messy mess. Write Pretty Hefty Moose, c/o Chief Plenty Hefty Pony, Ottawatamie Reservation, Pony Express Code 3, Feo Territorio.

UNRESPONSIVE TESTIMONIUMS

Unpeachable and steamable individuals of questionable character indicate their superior knowledge by indicating to the proprietor the tremendous antiquities experienced and joyous powers of fruitful and relaxing combustion relished with their appetites, diminished by ingesting savory nutrients at the Back 40.

I gained. . .from 35 lbs. to 200 lbs. I was an expert escape artist. Nothing was small enough to contain me. Then I began eatin' meals at the Back 40. Now I am 200 lbs. which fits my six foot frame. Now even the silent movin' picture folks want me for a cowboy hero, thanks to the Back 40.

Ronald (Skinny) Thinner

A notorious, mean, nasty villain, Seril (Cyril?) Slithery, who used to burn young maidens at the stake, tie up grandma's, steal kid's toys and play with them himself, and race 95 year old men to the john, was recently awarded the highest honor of the town by Mayor Rawlins for bravery beyond the call of human expectancy when he caught Grandma Twiddy jumping from the top floor of the hotel. (She weighed 350 lbs.) When asked what changed his disposition, he replied: "I ate some barbecue at the Back 40; it was so good that I have been plum tickled ever since, especially when it cost so little."

Mr. Proprietor, I was suffering from Blue rumanis with an added nervous twitch due to my wife's Indian-style cooking. Possum' fat boiled in ranch style beans stuffed in armadillo garnished with diced crickets ain't my idee' of nourishment, especially for three square meals a day. That's why I come in from the hills every night for that delicious Back 40 B.B.Q., and no indigestion. My Best Regards, Hill Man Henry Miller. Itchville, Montana.

Toothless Tomroy, known around town as Whistler, was never known to eat in public, due to his leaving large portions of food all over the eating area. It was embarassing since his mouth, which was toothless, couldn't quite hold onto whatever he was eating. On Tuesday of last week he was seen comin' out of the Back 40. Toothless said he downed a whole meal without spillin' nary a crumb for the first time in 40 years 'cause the Back 40 B.B.Q. was so tender. Now he always eats at the Back 40, but still whistles.

Fig. 7 Menu cover, The Back Forty Restaurant.

received a large package bearing the restaurant name. The package contained copies of the paper, a large ceramic serving dish with my name on it, plus a letter detailing what had occurred since our meeting. Their catering business had multiplied six times in dollar volume. Local industry made a visit by guests a must. They had just finished a special printing in tabloid form of all their recipes and were thinking about a brochure with illustrations of the farms and of historical sites. Local and national public relations staffs of local industry constantly mailed in news items and were holding sales meetings at this inn, for its newsworthiness, as against the impersonality of major hotels. They were receiving a constant flow of news from organizations in the city.

Each restaurant has its own "acres of diamonds" but this treasure trove will only be unearthed by hard thinking about concepts and by followthrough. The success of the menu does not depend on how much money is expended, or on how costly the art and preparation; it depends on management working on "the look" to sell their customers and give excitement to their business. The phrases "I'll have the usual" or "even the flyspecks are the same" ultimately doom the establishment.

Remaining vibrant and alive means working at changing menus at least twice annually, and having a consistent pattern of new presentations for special events, holidays, and local situations. The amount of available material is staggering, yet the number of operations using these sources is limited. It is one matter to have the reference sources, another to possess the initiative to use the information to best advantage. Some useful sources are:

A. Each major country has national trade commissions in most large cities, whose sole purpose is to publicize that country's products. Therefore, black and white and color photos, posters, and background historical material are yours at no cost. Many countries go so far as to have magnificent full-color menu covers available for overprinting. Recipes and literature are also to be had, segments of which may be used to authenticate dishes offered on your menu.

B. Trade associations have files that provide a flood of information, including stock menu covers, illustrations, and recipes. There is no end to the number of these groups—fruit, poultry, fish, beef, wine, spirits. All have reams of material suitable for reproduction and welcome your requests. The U.S. Department of Agriculture, state agriculture departments, and public information bureaus are all cooperative.

C. Libraries and the files of major newspapers and magazines are another source of art. A case in point. For example, the owner of a small Italian restaurant went to the library of the local university. For $3.65 he had xerox copies made of illustrations of ancient Roman feasts and Bacchanals. The name of his restaurant was "The Bacchanal"—and he named each specialty after a famous Roman.

D. Public relations departments of major corporations will often work with you on special event planning—furnishing art and research.

E. Airlines, transportation companies, and other major carriers have fabulous menu covers available, prints, reproduction material, flags, and an endless array of exciting promotional aids that can produce a worldly and charming menu. In exchange, they would expect a reproduction of their aircraft or logo somewhere on the menu.

The list is as broad as your imagination. Libraries are a major material source, second-hand bookstores have old books packed with illustrations that are provocative. Our philosophy is that the world is full of marvelous ideas that are waiting to be used; few take advantage of their potential.

3

LANGUAGE

Fascinating menu copy charms a customer into an extra purchase, and makes stealing a few calories seem only right. The use of words can produce confidence in the chef, the management, and the establishment. Words will make food a joy, a romance, an affair; words can seduce the toughest customer into trying the most delicate of gourmet delights. The lack of appropriate words, or inability to glamourize, can detract from the overall quality and professionalism of the menu. Here are examples of taking the ordinary and turning a phrase that makes serving an exciting event:

An oyster house: "The story is told that Caesar would send wagons to the snow-capped moutains, load them with snow and then, manned by his finest charioteers, rush the fresh snow to the shores where the oysters were taken. Packing the oysters in the snow, the chariots would race to the Emperor, who could then enjoy this sea treasure at its finest moment.

"Diamond Jim would have loved our freshly iced oysters. He would have his oysters packed in barrels of ice, handed over to a waiting freight that would highball to New York City; there, the restaurant had a swift moving carriage to make the final delivery, so that Diamond Jim, Lily Langtry, and friends would be properly fed.

"We don't ask our customers to do more than be seated at our oyster bar—we'll deliver fresh selected oysters safely on your plate, packed in ice, ready to be enjoyed."

Coffee shop in Detroit: "Have you ever thought about the word 'breakfast'? Literally, it means the first meal of the day. The palate is clean, the stomach empty, the head clear.

"We work hard to break the fast, to make every taste worthy of your presence. Our juices are sparkling with freshness, our coffee gurgles with joy, our eggs are cuddly and warm, our bakers have spent the night worrying over your muffins and danish. Our bacon, sausage, and ham are freshly sliced and wrapped to be certain they are at their moistened best.

"Our waitresses get up extra early to be wide awake and cheerful, and our cashier, well, you've got to get up real early to beat her. We wish you a fresh start—and welcome to a hearty breaking of the fast."

A fast food operation: "We dislike calling our fried chicken 'fried chicken.' It's much, much more. Our chickens are so very fresh you hear the 'clucks'—we lace our batter with fresh milk, and then pause for a moment and give thanks to Marco Polo. For we add exotic spices, herbs, and seasonings. Then we slowly and gently whip the batter to a lather, and into this rich blend we place a chicken breast, a leg, a thigh.

"Our chefs are so enraptured by the magnificence of the aroma that on occasion we use brute force to take these golden brown treasures from them. But—we handle them carefully, no bruising, no shaking—we depend on our trained self-control to bring our wonderous chicken platters to your table."

A world-famous restaurant on New York's Second Avenue sells their hors d'oeuvres: "We could rave on and on and tell you the wonders we perform. Whether you say Antipasto, or in Swedish, Smorgasbord, in German, Vorspeise, or even Zakouska from Russia, or try to be cute and request appeteasers, we really don't mind—for there are no words to describe the exotic delicacies we present to start your meal."

Think of these examples and then turn their philosophy to your establishment, to your specialties, your servings. The right words

St. James Hotel   **November 22, 1893.**

❖ MENU ❖

Oysters or Clams 25

SOUPS
Consommé, Louisiana 25 40   Giblet à l'irlandaise 30 50
Soldat victorieux 25 40   Cream of celery, duchesse 30 50
Purée de gibier, St. Hubert 30 50
Tomate au riz 20 35   Split pea 20 30

SIDE DISHES
Hot: Cromesquis de volaille à la russe 75
Olives 20   Celery 40   Caviar 35   Sardines 30   Chutney 15
Radishes 25   Lyons sausage 35   Anchovies 30   Stuffed olives 30

FISH
Fried eels, tartar sauce 45   Filet of sole en turban, italienne 70   Pompano, virginienne 60
Salmon steak, French peas 75   Spanish mackerel, New Orleans 60   Whitebait 40
Smelts à l'étouffade 60   Oyster crabs on toast 75
Lobster, Courbet 75   Striped bass, oyster sauce 65

RELEVES
Roast sirloin of beef, sémoule brissotins 75   Boiled fowl with salt pork 75

ENTREES
Broiled filet of beef, Trianon 1 00   Spring chicken sauté, Parmentier 1 25
Paupiettes of veal glacé à l'oseille 60   Squab en crapaudine 1 00
Plover sauté, forestière 90   Fricassée of lamb's feet, champignons frais 60
Fresh mushrooms on toast 1 00   Terrapin, Maryland 2 00

ROAST
Ribs of beef 40 60   Lamb, mint sauce 60   Leg of mutton 30 50
Chicken, half 1 00   Spring turkey, cranberry sauce 75   Duckling, half 1 00

GAME
Canvas-back duck 3 50   Red-head duck 2 50   Teal duck 90   Mallard duck 1 50 75
Partridge 75 1 50   English snipe 75   Grouse 75 1 50   Plover 75   Reed birds 75
Quail 75   Woodcock 1 25   Squab 80

VEGETABLES
Brussels sprouts 45   French artichokes 50   Spinach 30   Cauliflower 40
Lima beans 25   Oyster-Bay asparagus 60   New string beans 30
Stuffed green peppers 40
Stewed tomatoes 25   Mashed turnips 25   Sweet corn 25   Succotash 30
French peas 40   Squash 20   American peas 25   Cèpes, Bordelaise 60
Macaroni, gratin 30   Spaghetti, Milanaise 50   Fried egg plant 25
Potatoes: Sarah Bernhardt 25   Sweet 25   Stewed 20
A l'Em Jay 25   Boiled 15   Mashed 15   Fried 15   Julienne 20   Parisienne 20
Hashed with cream 25   Croquettes 25   Duchesse 25   Anna 30   Lyonnaise 20

COLD
Spring turkey 75   Lamb 60   Partridge 75 1 50   Quail 75   Ribs of beef 40 60
Chicken, half 1 00   Boned capon 50 75   Plain lobster 60   Fresh salmon 60
Corned beef 40   Ham 25 40   Tongue 25 40   Lamb's tongue 25
Pâté de foie-gras 1 00
Salad: Tomatoes 50   Celery 50   Cucumber 40   Chicory 40   Lettuce 40
Watercress 25   Chicken 60 1 00   Lobster 50 75
Russe 60   Escarole 40   Macédoine 50   Anchovy 50   Shrimp 75

DESSERT
Hot: Vermicelli pudding 20   Omelette soufflée, vanille 50
Rice croquettes, lemon 30
Cold: Bread pudding 20   Port wine jelly 25   Fig tarts 20   Apricot pie 20
Cocoanut pie 20   D'Artois grillé aux confitures 25   Eclairs au chocolat 20
Charlotte glacée 35   Meringue glacée 35   Meringue à la crème 30   Carlsbad wafers 20
Pound cake 20   Fruit cake 20   Lady fingers 20   Macaroons 20   Petits fours 20
Charlotte Russe 25

ICE CREAM
Vanilla 25   Chocolate 25   Pistache 25   Mixed 30   Napolitaine 30   Tutti frutti 30
Strawberry 25   Biscuit glacé 30   Biscuit Tortoni 30   Nesselrode 35
Mousse aux fraises 40   Biscuits, diplomatic 40
Water Ice: Lemon 25   Raspberry 25   Oranges 25
Sorbets: Maraschino 35   Kirsch 35   Rum 35   A l'arrack 35   Lalla Rookh 35

CHEESE
Gorgonzola 25   Stilton 25   Brie 25   Roquefort 25
Gruyère 25   Gervais 25   Camembert 25   Neufchâtel 20   American 15

FRUITS
Peaches and cream 40   Pears 25
Pineapple 30   Apples 20   Bananas 20   Oranges 25   Grapes 30
Preserves: Raspberries, strawberries, green gages, quinces and damsons 30   Nuts and raisins 25
Bar le Duc 40   Marmalade 20   Apricot jam 25   Red currant jam 25   Figs 20
Demi-tasse 15

HALF PORTIONS SERVED TO ONE PERSON ONLY

Fig. 8 Menu from the St. James Hotel. Photo courtesy of Bohn-Bettoni Collection, University of Nevada, Las Vegas Library.

will give your menu items a refreshing new approach.

Whether you have a truck stop or a pizza palace, it is the extra descriptive word or phrase that takes your offerings out of the ordinary and gives them a flair and dash and presents your offerings in a way that bespeaks good taste and personality.

In Santa Monica a prize-winning Italian restaurant has a menu broken down by the food of each province. Next to these entries are fables and historical anecdotes. "Emilia Romagna: *Emilia*—where the making of pasta and the making of love are both forms of art; *Romagna*—fierce individualistic performance—but superb food. Here the story is told of the pasta maker who, through a keyhole, eyed the navel of a statue of Venus. The navel so inspired him that he created 'tortellini' in its shape. It has also inspired the sauce our chef prepares when you order our tortellini."

One seafood bar has set its entire menu in verse, borrowing the meter and rhyme of the *Rime of the Ancient Mariner.*

Some menus offer a peek into the forbidden areas of chefs' recipes for sauces and secrets of meal preparation.

A smattering of geography and history all add to a more masterful and credible menu:

"Our Black Forest Torte is the next best thing to a trip to that forest so famed in song and rhyme."

A step further is a mention of the chef, used here in an item description: "Our chef Robert was trained in France; we call it Duck with Orange, he calls it Canard à l'Orange." This one sentence announces to the guest that the chef is knowledgeable, and is authentically French, so that when the chef recommends the patron must be impressed.

GUIDELINES TO SHOWMANSHIP

The words that convey confidence must be your words. Clarity is foremost, simplicity follows. Write as you speak and customers will identify that this is your menu—and yours alone.

You know your customers, the prices they will pay, the words they are comfortable with in dining. When a cheese tray becomes

"Our Cheesy Platter," or simple ice cream becomes "Ice-Cream Creations," the customer chuckles and the cash register rings an extra sale.

Think on this. One menu states, "Veal Marsala," the other reads, "An Inspiration from Sicily—Veal Marsala: We take the whitest of young veal and immerse it in the great fortified wine of Sicily, Marsala, from the region whose name it bears. The endless troops that have crossed this rugged land have each left their impression, but none have tampered with Marsala of Sicily, the cooking wine par excellence, our *Veal Marsala* from Sicily to you."

Good menu reading takes nothing for granted. How many customers know that Marsala is a fortified wine, how many know that it is produced in Sicily?

A menu can give your patrons a feeling of being knowledgeable about food and its history as in these examples:

Sauce Zabayon: Introduced to the French court by Catherine de Medici of France, now introduced to you by *(name of restaurant)*.

Sauce Béarnaise: One of the great French sauce classics, named after King Henri IV of France, known as the Great Béarnais.

In New Orleans I discovered a menu with a magnificent illustration of Sir Francis Drake's defeat of the Spanish Armada. The caption read, "Thank Sir Francis Drake for our Calvados Sauce. In his hard-fought battle a vessel of Spain foundered ashore; its name was *Calvados*. This is the name that the apple brandy makers of Brittany gave to their very own apple brandy, distilled from cider. This is the secret ingredient we add to our hard sauce to make it worthy of your palate."

Does the British use of the ward "starters" have greater appeal than "appetizers"? Or does the Roman "Gustus Antecena" tell us more? Create your own phrase, "This is where the 'Man Who Came to Dinner' starts."

A great Chicago menu is worded completely as a theater program: *Prologue*—The history of the establishment. *Act I*—The appetizers. *Act II*—The Main Course. *Act III*—The Happy Ending.

There are a thousand and one themes that your imagination can produce. The art follows the theme, and suddenly your customers have a conversation piece. During the Lenten season, one eating place distributes its menu printed on the reverse side of a cut-out of a fish. The owner reproduces seven fish illustrations, each a different species. On the inside he tells his customers the delicacies of each type. On the reverse side panel he tells the story of Lent. It's a dramatic presentation that each year brings in a flood of requests for the complete series.

Let word magic work for you. Using just the heading "The Specialty of the House" on your menu is an incomplete presentation. Give the why and where as well. Is there an entree that takes extra preparation? Explain the process. Are your steaks aged? Give the customer the reason why. Does your establishment have a heritage, a history? Then tell the story. Let your menu be so convincing, so readable, that every visitor will recall your restaurant not only by the food and service, but by its originality. Your food servers will be proud to present a menu that is thoughtfully and tastefully executed. Your chef will add suggestions to make his dishes representative of his talent. All these assets for better communication with your patrons are yours.

4

SPECIALTY MENUS

There are many types of food service operations that cater to a special or limited clientele. The menu can be an important tool for attracting and keeping these customers. This chapter discusses how some specialty operations can create specialty menus.

THE CHILDREN'S WORLD

There are two means of displaying the menu category of food for children. It can appear on the menu itself, or in a separate form that has a double use, both as a menu and as a device to keep the young set occupied and amused.

With the growing number of working mothers and single parents, menus for their offspring take on a vital significance. To attract the business of the parents, the restaurant must illustrate, through their menus, their capability and desire to serve the younger market. Tied in with this must be the availability of proper furniture and the ability of staff to manage the problems of serving children. In certain casino operations the menu for children is carefully present-

Fig. 9 Cover of children's menu, Gardens Restaurant. Photo courtesy of University of Nevada, Las Vegas Library.

ed to illustrate the restaurants' interest in children. The parent is thus made to feel comfortable in the environment.

Many devices developed from a realistic approach to children's inability to read are available to keep them busy. Pictures that represent the food, games that involve coloring, cut-outs, and puzzles are all possible. The child's interests can find expression in the form of cartoons, booklets, crayons, and souvenirs. Bibs, plastic implements, buttons, and balloons are happy reminders of your restaurant. McDonald's has certainly demonstrated its abilities in merchandising food to children as a key to success.

One of the great children's marketing concepts by a family-style restaurant is that of the king and queen cut-out. The parent is presented with a large booklet of instructions. The folder has a crown, a scepter, stars, and medals. As the child completes each segment of the meal, he or she is given a different ornament. On completion of the meal, the child is crowned by the server.

Fig. 10 Inside of children's menu, Gardens Restaurant. Photo courtesy of University of Nevada, Las Vegas Library.

Printing their menu on a balloon for children has provided something of a walking billboard for one unit. In a Minneapolis restaurant, creativity is at work: A series of placemats combines the menu with games. One illustrates a farmer and his products in the fashion of a storybook. An Oklahoma restaurant advises parents that they have a library of books that is open for their use.

At a major hotel in London, a room service tent states, "We care about your children." The tent advises that special diets can be followed in their kitchen, that smaller portions of most menu listings are available, and that the staff understands and wishes to assist so that all will enjoy their meals.

Many who take an aggressive position list the brand name of the foods they stock for infants in jars, and infant cereals. The child of today is exposed to a greater variety of foods than ever before, and the basic children's menu offerings of frankfurter, hamburger, and leg of chicken is not sufficient.

The availability of interest-grabbing tools is fundamental in capturing the market. A simple folder with an accordion fold becomes self-standing. With the menu in the center, and eye-catching illustrations on the left and right, management has a marvelous opportunity to sell itself and its performance. The ultimate creative piece ties together menu presentation and functional service. These pieces need not be costly, it is the content that makes for success rather than concentration on color and artwork.

"We'll warm your bottle—or chill your juice" is the opening line on a menu at one restaurant that welcomes children. The working mother or single parent, having spent a trying day, chooses a place to eat that accepts children graciously. The executive who takes the family to dinner will be captured by menus he or she recalls welcoming children.

Staff training and understanding are vital in adding to and maintaining this area of business. A school of restaurant and hotel management has recently prepared a guide, reflecting the opportunities that exist for this growth market.

One eating place has the cutest idea yet—it presents parents with a Polaroid photo of them at dinner with their children. Each photo is presented in a frame that bears the restaurant name. The parent is simultaneously requested to fill out a card that gives data on the child, such as birth date, age, and eating likes and dislikes. The owner informs me that each child receives a birthday card and holiday card. He traces specific business to this program—families coming in for birthdays and other occasions. Parents constantly comment when they return that these reminders are most important to them.

Creativity will be productive in this phase. It involves the performance of the entire restaurant. The astute dining establishment at every price range and position must appreciate the importance to the total business the children's market represents.

WINE GOURMET DINNERS

Some restaurants have used the growing interest in wine to create "Wine Gourmet Dinners." This is an offering of a comprehensive gourmet meal, including wine, that must be ordered at least one week in advance.

One Atlantic City hotel set aside a specific table for this treatment. Originally only one table was in use; this has now grown to three tables nightly, with plans to apply the entire room to it.

When the host of a party interested in the wine gourmet dinner comes to discuss the meal, the manager shows a display of famous menus from special occasions. He also has a collection of special dishes and talks about the restaurant or chef that created the meal.

For many years one eating place used its cellar for storage. Seeing the possibility of tying in with the growing interest in wine, they converted the space into a wine cellar, which because of its small size, is used for private parties. The walls are decorated with bottles, the table is a tasting table from a winery, and the chairs are made of the staves of wine barrels. No electric light is used, only candles. A printed brochure is available that carries the name of the host and the occasion.

Probably the most impressive means of selling the wine gourmet dinner is used by a New Orleans restaurant in its menu clip-ons. The illustrated copy names a gourmet recipe and follows through by commenting that during normal service, the staff works hard to turn out fine cuisine, but by planning a party in advance, it is possible to have the foods of the great chefs such as the menu illustrates. A reservation line with room for name, address, and phone number appears at the bottom.

As the interest in exotic and ethnic food grows, it provides a stimulus for the restaurateur. To those who find the culinary arts a springboard to establishing a better position in the local market, this is an exciting challenge to be accepted at every level and type of dining room.

SELF-SERVICE BUFFETS

Imagine a huge, six-foot-long, four-foot-wide panel, mounted and framed in split logs, with a three-foot-long fork and spoon beside it. The menu is in the center of the panel. A slide at the bottom can be changed to accommodate the special of the day. This is a buffet menu designed for Yellowstone Park, in keeping with the wood decor of the dining room.

A Las Vegas buffet features a table mat with the caption, "Don't Gamble." Underneath is a layout that indicates foods that are available and where they are to be found.

A new innovation is the salad bar, and here there are several novel turns. One restaurant lists its salad bar "For Nature Lovers Only." Another restaurant features the "organically grown vegetarian collection," with a display alongside explaining the manner in which this method of growing functions. Another innovation is the "make your own dressing" concept. Table mats list recipes for dressings and guests are invited to create their own.

In Atlantic City, a major buffet offers the services of two chefs who work over burners at the end of a table surrounded by a variety of ingredients—capers, lox, liver, onions, etc. Guests are given a list of suggested omelets, and ingredients for egg dishes that are available, ending with—bright idea—"Name your choice."

One eatery that has a total seafood buffet varies their ice carvings with ships, porpoises, and mermaids. The carvings hold a gigantic seashell, inside of which is lettered the types of seafood available that day.

A dramatic buffet presentation is the international "Pick-Your-Country" buffet, as presented by a major hotel in San Francisco. Each day, the food of a different country is offered. Huge flags hang from the ceiling; smaller flags are set on each table. The menu is presented listing the specialties of the country, showing the region and history of each dish.

In Cheyenne, Wyoming, a diner offers a "Breakfast Chow Down." Guests are given a menu that carries the expected weather, stock prices, and other information.

New York's Chinatown has a restaurant that presents a "Chinateria" in which chefs work in the center of a ring-shaped table while guests circle it choosing items. The unique menu not only contains a wide variety of authentic foods—but has a great plus. The guest may fill out the bottom of the menu with a suggestion for a dish he or she would like to have served in the future at the restaurant. The reverse side is "Fortune Cookie Fever" which lists the foods preferred by people born under different astrological signs and the significance of the signs. The menu is printed on rice paper.

Probably the most efficient buffet—part of a growing trend—is one where the guest is presented with a brochure. Each buffet item is listed and explained. Next to each there is a box to be marked. The diner may either view and select in person or present the list to the server who brings the food. On the opposite page, doodlers are invited to play while waiting. The top of the page explains various doodles and their significance.

I know of only two "Sandwich Buffets." At one, the guest is furnished with a list of favorite sandwiches that have been created by well-known customers. There is an enormous variety of breads, cold cuts, and condiments. The menu cover portrays the Earl of Sandwich and explains the many theories on how the sandwich was born. In a semihumorous manner are listed the do's and don'ts of successful sandwich making, with suggested sandwiches for senior citizens, for cowboys, for police officers, etc. The success of this buffet is beyond belief; it is now open twenty-four hours a day.

The buffet menu is vital to moving traffic and maintaining volume. The customer must know what is available and where it is located to avoid time-consuming questions. Prices must be clear; if there are added costs, these must be stated.

To discourage the plate overloader from taking more than he or she will eat, some buffets add cartoons to their menus, with captions like "Take as much as you like—but eat what you take," "Is this trip necessary?" (illustrating an overloaded car), and "What you leave over gives our chef a hangover."

Encouraging guests to dispose of the waste on their plates themselves brings them into the orbit of "helping out"—and is not resented, but appreciated. Many will go out of their way to pitch in.

Some restaurants offer wine on an "as much as you like" basis. One Italian restaurant in Las Vegas offers as much wine as you wish. The owner states that with very few exceptions, customers will only drink a normal quantity, and that in many cases on the second round will apologize and ask for half a carafe.

One of the great restaurants in the South decided to gamble on their Sunday Champagne Brunch. They placed bottles on display and suggested that diners serve themselves. Skeptics were certain that diners would take the bottles to their tables. On the contrary, guests respected the honor system, and complimented the owner. The only other comment was, "Do the same with wine." The table menu simply stated, "Have a sparkling Sunday—we're glad you're here. The champagne is on the house."

Revenue in food buffets can be built up by the use of table tents to apprise customers of the price of beverages, for splits and half bottles, and by the glass.

A prominent Chicago buffet provides a wide variety of beers, wines, and ales. It offers champagne in splits and 6.4-ounce sizes, all screw-capped for self-serving.

With the shopping mall as a part of our life-style comes the grouping of eating places in one area—an exciting concept. Creativity can be reflected in the common display that posts lists of the food available from the different outlets, with a daily menu of the specials. Seating is normally in the center, and shoppers can create their own buffet by visiting each booth separately. Portland, Seattle, New York, Los Angeles, and many other cities have farmers' markets and other areas where individual food stalls together make up a buffet of sorts. Those on the Monterey and San Francisco piers were probably among the earliest to develop. Here, by walking through the street, the diner can find a tremendous array of food. The earthy aromas and appetizing arrangements form an outdoor buffet.

The pushcarts of lower Manhattan in the early nineteen hundreds offered ethnic foods, both hot and cold. By traversing the length of the street an adventurer could sample and enjoy a complete meal.

From the French and Italians we learned the joy of food on wheels. Progressing from the simple hot-dog vendor, we now have French crepes, and Chinese and Oriental delicacies available this way. In Japan, the hot plate on wheels puts together noodles, onions, and peppers in a national dish.

Possibly the first commercial form of buffet was New York's Horn & Hardart Automat. Here the food was exposed to the customer through a window with coin slots alongside. After inserting nickels, he or she would open the window and remove the food. Hot dishes were available as well from a group of open steam tables. Here, the food was shown and the explanations were clear and fixed.

Visual presentation is not the total answer; the buffet must be merchandised to achieve a romance of its own. Blackboards, easel displays, news bulletins are all part of the total immediate service preparation.

Unless the buffet dishes are explained we have a mobile mess. The creativity factor provides speed and eliminates waste. Whether the explanation appears on an overhead that hangs downward, or on the front of a pan, questions must be answered.

To fully explain the rotation of their offerings, a Florida restaurant gives the customer a weekly calendar of foods that will be prepared. On the calendar are other significant dates, holidays, historical dates, and astrological data.

The focus on presentation and display is the key to success of this operation. Newspaper- and almanac-type layout gives the guest the food information.

While eliminating the irritants and annoyances of waiting and tipping, in most cases buffets provide very little server attention, and therefore the printed piece is the prime connecting point between management and guest. A world of ideas are being used for this. One carries a detailed illustration of the steam and cold tables, making known exactly what will fill those dishes.

The buffet is here. Imagination and merchandising will precipitate new names and new strengths. This is a field in transition, one where the potential of exploitation will bring forth new success stories.

THE CATERING CONCEPT

The dramatic changes that have occurred in the field of catering show it to be possibly the most imaginative area in the food service industry.

Today, the scope of catering operations ranges from small mobile units to gourmet sit-down dinners for five thousand. The catering director of a major chain pointed out the increasing sophistication of the catering market by turning to a glass-enclosed cabinet on his wall. The case was filled with bottles of wine and champagne. His potential customers not only want to know the wines they will be using, but demand a tasting. "In the food field, customers are growing more selective and are insulted if I even discuss chicken and roast beef," he says. Decorations are demanded, ice carvings, floral arrangements, and color schemes are closely watched and discussed.

The abrupt change in catering concepts has been brought about through travel, television, and the growing knowledge and interest in gourmet dining. To capture the market and be competitive, one catering chain has developed a presentation by categories. They have a gourmet section that contains such dishes as coq au vin, steak tartare, Cornish game hen, duck à l'orange, and a host of other dishes. Hors d'oeuvres selections are more worldly; Chinese, Japanese, and European dishes are listed. Price is secondary, service is important. Desserts such as crepes suzette and strawberries Romanoff are gradually replacing layer cake, ice cream, and ices.

One gourmet catering service finds that the private party catering business has a new look—more worldly, with much more knowledgeable patronage. They cater many parties where the wine is purchased by the party giver, who also prepares the menu and turns it over to them for action, or for remarks and suggestions.

Often, the theme is the thing, whether it's one with some sort of representation, or simply the use of a unifying color. The theme must be carried out in every detail, from place settings to wall hangings to the type of meal served.

A Seattle restaurant that prizes its catering reputation tells of the ocean liner captain whose wedding they handled. The centerpiece was a ten-foot tinted model of the liner and the entire room was done in blue and gold. Each course was a different type of seafood. Each wine and champagne was from a country where the ship docked. The final cordial was crème de menthe garnished with a green cherry, served over ice to resemble the ocean. The menu was in the form of a ship's log, listing the time and place the couple met, their first date, engagement, etc., as well as dishes served. Under "Ship's Personnel" the names of the minister and family members were given as well.

The caterer must have available an entire collection of menu covers with settings to cover each and every occasion. With more women working, the time span for wedding preparation is less than ever. Plans for catering spontaneous situations must also be incorporated in the presentation book.

The demand by industrial organizations for inside serving is growing. The alert caterer finds out as soon as possible about the occasion and the level of sophistication and experience of those who will attend. When a major New York bank chartered an aircraft to host a group of foreign banking executives to a resort area, the diligent caterer analyzed the list and was convinced that the best way to satisfy all was with a completely American menu and wine list. It worked. He served ham and eggs, turkey, and apple pie with the wines of California and champagnes from New York. All guests were supplied with menus showing where the servings originated. Lunch was fresh salmon flown in from Oregon, fresh fruit, and cheese.

Airline catering systems are in the most difficult position— plagued by economy drives and a demand for a differential in first class and economy serving. The stringent constraints of the situation have stimulated ingenuity in many forms. The serving of a box of chocolates on one carrier adds a festive note. A major midwestern carrier offers a wine booklet that makes excellent reading and constantly offers a new and varied selection of wines.

Planners of a huge convention looked for a method of feeding their attendees that would not keep them off the convention floor. The caterer prepared five groups of sandwiches and made them up into plates. Each offering contained three different half sandwiches, with one group all deli, another seafood (sardines, tuna, salmon). A large table was set up with fruit, cheese, and pies. The varied food pleased all, and the menu provided a complete numbered list that explained what was in the three-in-one platters.

Given a difficult budget to meet, one catering service served the lowly pizza and all the trimmings along with spaghetti with a choice of three sauces. It was a do-it-yourself situation for the guests. The wine, in three gallon jugs, was also "help yourself." A fact sheet on compatible "get togethers" served as a menu. The party was a smash success on a very low budget.

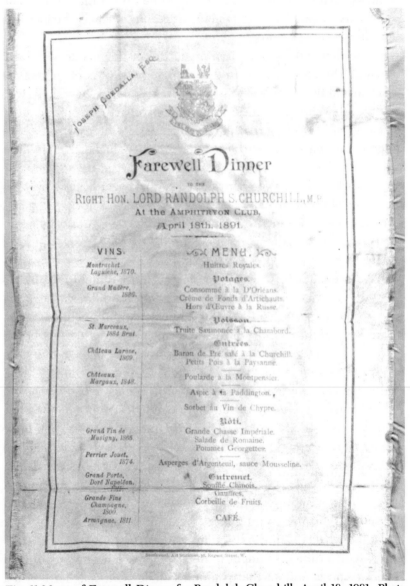

Fig. 11 Menu of Farewell Dinner for Randolph Churchill, April 18, 1981. Photo courtesy of Bohn-Bettoni Collection, University of Nevada, Las Vegas Library.

The inventiveness of the caterer can often make an inexpensive party an unforgettable event. One Christmas a large company wanted a party that would be unique, with unusual food, all in the full spirit of the holiday. The caterer responded with the pastries and the traditional holiday dishes of many nations. The guests were supplied with a brochure that explained the derivation of each dish, and gave the recipes. The number of letters received by the caterer was incredible; many of the dishes had brought back memories to the guests.

There is a new group of caterers who prize their coordination of theme and food. Their concept is a complete presentation that covers all phases of the event, planning unique food, wine, and service. From the selection of the food servers' costume through to the menu, all must fit.

A major Italian wine company was at a loss for an original party idea. Their competitors all used the white-tie approach at fine hotels, with luxurious food. The hotel director they approached created a situation that will not be forgotten for a long while. As the guests arrived, they were led to a dressing room. The men were given togas, the women a choice of dancing-girl costume or Roman-type sari. All food was served as the guests reclined, while the wine was poured from amphoras. The food was brought into the room by "slaves," and the entertainment was as authentic as possible. The emcee was accompanied by a trained lion. Menus matched the setting. Written in Latin with English translations, they were printed on parchment-like paper, rolled up, tied with purple ribbon and sealed with a wax signet. Such showmanship takes the full creativity of the catering staff—but is worth the expended energy.

The larger the group, the more attention to detail the caterer must spend to retain the personal feeling that the host and hostess seek. A demand made to a caterer in Detroit that the dinner be "the kind of party that everyone dreams of attending" was answered in the following effective manner. The room was surrounded by mirrors. The servers wore powdered wigs, and each guest received a menu that explained that the dinner was the very same as one given at Versailles by Madame Pompadour. The champagne and wine were the same types as had been served.

Drama plays an integral part in success; effective research establishes the ability of the catering organization to fulfill the desires of the client.

A Columbus Day fête had fluorescent mobiles of the *Nina, Pinta,* and *Santa Maria*: an Italian flag was intertwined with them. The menu tassel was in the flag colors, and the menu cover was a reproduction of a map of the world made during the time of Columbus. On the inside cover was a biography of Columbus. The servers' outfits were characteristic of the period. The food was created from a period menu discovered at the University of Milan. The different wines were poured in turn from large amphoras carried by women in costume. A quartet playing fifteenth-century musical instruments performed during dinner.

A caterer in Hawaii was challenged with a golden wedding anniversary. The couple had spent most of their life on the island, and their friends were of a multitude of nationalities. Guests were invited to attend in authentic national costumes and a gay luau was to be served. The caterer recognized the problems of seating on benches or on the ground, since most of the guests were in their senior years. He rented comfortable beach chairs and constructed, in the form of surfboards, planks that fit completely across the chair arms. Each plank had the initials of the hosts, and after the party it became a souvenir. The drinks were served in cut coconuts. The front cover of the menu was based on James Michener's book, *Hawaii,* and the inside related the history of the couple and what they had accomplished during their time on Hawaii. The leis were unique—interspersed with the flowers were reproductions of gold wedding rings. The dessert, made partially of ice, was a smoldering volcano.

Catering service planning is increasingly dependent on the caterer's creativity. Gourmet demands have only begun. A greater knowledge of wines and spirits is necessary.

Calorie-conscious individuals, natural food enthusiasts, and those with religious dietary restrictions may prefer not to dine than to go back on their nutrition beliefs. The informative menu that supplies calorie counts, and advises what is available can be very important to guests relying on catered food. One serving company publishes a week's menu each Monday. The diners thus have time to plan when they will eat out. The booklet has a coupon asking for advice on any special foods that may be desired.

The caterer can take advantage of the new interest in gourmet cooking and create menus to emphasize the gourmet concept. The newsworthiness of the *Nouvelle Cuisine* of Paul Bocuse has prompted many companies to distribute menus at affairs with full recipes credited to the Master Chef, along with the calorie count.

Mobile catering units have developed distinctive menu styles. One group of vets banded together to form a catering operation. They hand out a schedule of where they will be at a given time, and the menu they offer to local clubs, churches, and groups. They also list a series of phone numbers where they can be reached in the evening. Many vans carry a blackboard menu on one side, listing local sports scores below. Recognizable color schemes and pictorial renderings all work for identity.

ROOM SERVICE

There was a time when room service clientele was limited to the elegant and the wealthy, and to the business executive.

We now have a new clientele using this service. Needs now are different than they were in the past. Therefore, the new room service brochure must take into consideration the single traveler as well as the in-room business meetings, and their specific needs.

The traveling executive will be staying for longer periods and working out of his or her room. He or she will rely on the phone, and spend lengthier periods in the room. Therefore, the menu must be budget minded and have greater variety than before, and the food must be served in the most compact manner. Splits of wine, cans of beer, and individual bottled cocktails, all for single service, will become a must.

Printed material, numbered with plain pricing, and complete convenient meals that do not interfere with working material are a consideration for the executive involved in a working meeting.

For the in-room meeting, a series of recommendations for

specific numbers should be readable, presentable, and econom-
ically priced. The printed information must be clearly illustrated
and priced to avoid time-consuming delays. Baskets or trays should
be removed as quickly as possible.

To develop traffic in the hotel's better restaurant area, Early
Bird Breakfasts and dinners are effective. Coupons placed in rooms
offering a free glass of wine are effective traffic builders. A giveaway
cocktail during the Happy Hour will encourage customers to stay for
dinner.

Menus and printed material for special meals should wherever
possible give service-minded information: airline numbers, rental
cars, theater schedules, or a map of the business area, are all
compatible with the functional needs of the business traveler. A list
of business services, such as copying services, public secretaries,
etc., are time-saving helps that are appreciated.

THE TAKEOUT MENU

In-house office meetings of management and committees provide a source of income for the alert food server in the area of takeout food. By distributing a menu, he or she lets the audience know
that this service is available.

The takeout menu must be designed to avoid questions and
page turning. The menu should apply for a minimum of one week.
The other services—party catering, off-premise food serving—will
only develop by virtue of consistent announcements.

The "takeout" restaurant offers a world of potential to create a
simpatico feeling with the customer; but too few understand the
value any degree of consideration carries in customer goodwill. The
operator will normally have a listing of foods available on a pre-
printed order form.

In Detroit, a well-established coffee shop made a decision to go
after the takeout market. The owner felt that to work effectively
against competition he had to establish confidence in quality,
quickly. A simple brochure was prepared that cost no more than a
list. It had a brief history of the coffee shop, photos of the kitchen and
chef; each menu item had its own panel, with photo and description.

The result was a business increase so substantial that doubling the staff was necessary.

THE MILITARY WORLD

There are two distinct schools of thought involving menu planning for the military club system. One side believes that themes should be explicitly military; the other believes that, in order to compete with local establishments, the club decor and menu treatment should be non-military. Basically the best approach is individualized, where each club has a creative menu that fills the specific needs of the group that it serves.

One tactic, to capture the pride of the club and the base, is to illustrate the personality in whose honor the site was named and supply a history of the base. Focusing on historic landmarks associated with the area can be a creative tactic. Old illustrations or photos that show the base as it was at its inception, reproductions of groups of soldiers in the uniform of their time, early versions of aircraft, vessels, and weaponry, can all be used to individualize the menu.

The home of the Thunderbirds, a selected flying team of the air force located in Las Vegas, structured a dual message. The cover illustrated the aircraft on the base. Inside, each entrée was named with a phrase associated with gambling: "Pit Boss Burger," "Hi-Roller Chili," etc. The Air Force Academy in Colorado Springs, Colo., carried illustrations of the ranch on which it was constructed. The chapel and other points of interest were sketched on back covers. Yokota Air Force Base displayed its rock garden and sketches of Geisha costumes. Naija Hotel, in Korea, carried a splendid rendition of a Korean pagoda on the cover. The structured stones of Guam, the Rock and the early Spanish bridge are used. One club presented a map of the area with a flag indicating the base location.

An illustration of parallel thinking was the menus used by Bolling and Fort Sills. The Washington base depicted the development of aircraft from early versions to the modern. The artillery base, Fort Sills, pictured their branch in various ways, going back to the Spanish American war.

One of the most dramatic covers was created by the Admiral

WHITEMAN
AIR FORCE BASE

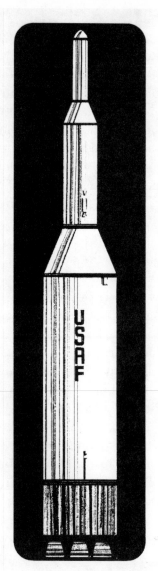

Non Commissioned
Officers Club

Fig. 12   Menu cover, Whiteman Air Force Base Non Commissioned Officers Club.

Kidd Club of San Diego. The Congressional Medal of Honor and the accomplishments of the admiral were pictured along with his portrait. An NCO club showed the rank stripes of its members in flight formation. Whiteman AFB in Missouri, using a dignified gatefold opening for its menu, has a picture of a missile in flight (See Fig. 12). In the other direction, the military base at Virginia Beach uses a photo of the beach, and Wright Patterson, Dayton, Ohio has a bird's eye panoramic view of the field. The marine site at Pendelton in Oceanside, California has a splendid red and gold design on the menu front cover that incorporates the Marine Corps insignia. The back cover shows various stages of uniform development. The officers clubs' menus tend to be more flamboyant, the NCO clubs' tend to stress their insignia, as they are more involved with the base and the work it performs. Enlisted personnel clubs' menus are simpler. Format planning is essential. Format planning allows the club to combine a civilian approach with a military tradition. One unit has duplicated the local paper's bannerhead, prints the menu on news stock, and announces club events in a calendar on the back cover. Inside is news about the base and its personnel. The ghosting technique in particular enables the design to be civilian with a background of military. The flow of personnel world-wide gives importance to foreign dishes. Many clubs present the dish in the native language.

Some menus use military language to describe dishes. The B-52 Burger defines the burger in bomber talk. The Deck Watch Dog—"ready in a flash"—tells a quick service story. The Sub-Sub needs no explanation. "Wing and a Prayer" was a surprise dish; the diner was certain of a wing, everything else was a guess. The "Hash Mark Hassle" was an NCO version of the mixed grill. "Gold Braid" Special was lobster tail and steak. "At Ease" was a dessert menu, "Parade Dress" entrées. "Trimming the Jib," a diet platter. Tying in with the specifics of their service, captions and courses sometimes appeared as signal flags, Morse code, or semaphores.

Wine is vital to the interest of the menu, since many military personnel stationed at European posts have acquired a high degree of wine knowledge. While most officers' clubs stress their wine list, NCO clubs and enlisted clubs feature the "popular" wines and beer, with a limited wine list. Carafe wine sales are popular in all clubs. Wine lists need be explained more carefully in non-officers' clubs. The use of the bin number system simplifies ordering. Brief but precise explanations of wine characteristics are necessary.

As many customers of clubs are singles or accompanied by a guest, it is advisable to maintain a selection of splits and half bottles. For members who are younger such wines as Lambrusco, Sangria, and cold duck are a must. Cordials and mixed drinks produced with cordials must be merchandised through the device of menu clip-ons and tents. The name alone is not sufficient; recipes should be displayed. Coordination between club lists and availability at package stores is functional.

Maintaining a flow of interest calls for ingenuity. By serving the food of different nations, tying in with the native wines, and decorating with flags and maps of the country involved, the club takes on a new look with each occasion. Colorful native costumes add to authenticity. The average base has a number of persons from each country who would be proud and pleased to help with the planning and preparation of special events.

Wine tastings are great fund raisers for various club-based organizations. Many of the organizations of wholesalers and wine importers will happily present a wine tasting. This may be used to cultivate sales by offering the wines tasted for immediate sale on the premises. The wine list should remain intact; but the concept of presenting new wines through displays is worthwhile in maintaining constant interest.

As the potential customer at a wine tasting is almost completely lost in details, the more clearly the information is presented, the greater the response. For demonstration purposes complete kits of all material provided should be at hand.

The movement into wine and cheese tastings calls for specifics in what will be provided, what the corkage charges are, and what services will be supplied. A decision that varies with each club concerns those individuals who would like to furnish their own wine or beer. The option, as the wine boom grows, is one that must be carefully weighed. Is a corkage charge in the best interests of the club? A base in California takes the back cover of its menu to discuss

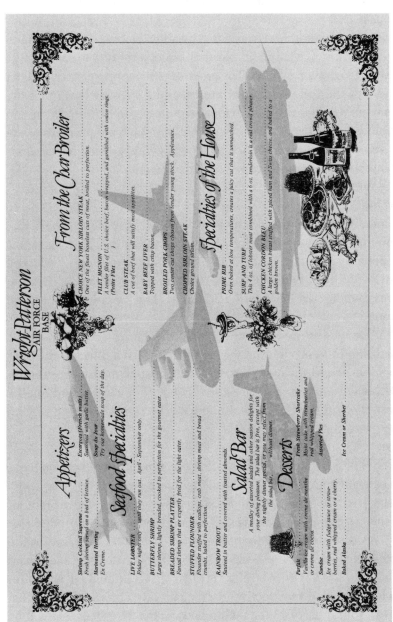

Wright-Patterson
AIR FORCE
BASE

Appetizers

Shrimp Cocktail Supreme ....
Fresh shrimp served on a bed of lettuce.

Escargot (French snails) ....
Sautéed with garlic butter.

Marinated Herring

Soup du Jour
Try our homemade soup of the day.

En Creme.

Seafood Specialties

LIVE LOBSTER .... until they run out. April - September only.
Friday nights only —

BUTTERFLY SHRIMP ....
Large shrimp, lightly breaded, cooked to perfection for the gourmet eater.

BREADED SHRIMP PLATTER ....
Fantail shrimp that are expertly fried for the light eater.

STUFFED FLOUNDER ....
Flounder stuffed with scallops, crab meat, shrimp meat and bread crumbs, baked to perfection.

RAINBOW TROUT
Sautéed in butter and covered with toasted almonds.

Salad Bar

A medley of assorted salads and other season delights for your dining pleasure. The salad bar is free, except with the nightly dinner special, or you may select from the salad bar without dinner.

Deserts

Parfait ....
Vanilla ice cream with creme de menthe or creme de cocoa.

Fresh Strawberry Shortcake
Moist cake with strawberries and real whipped cream.

Sundae ....
Ice cream with fudge sauce or straw-berries, real whipped cream or a cherry.

Assorted Pies

Baked Alaska

Ice Cream or Sherbet

From the Char Broiler

CHOICE NEW YORK SIRLOIN STEAK ....
One of the finest boneless cuts of meat, broiled to perfection.

FILET MIGNON ....
A tender filet of U.S. choice beef, bacon wrapped, and garnished with onion rings.
(Petite Filet)

CLUB STEAK ....
A cut of beef that will satisfy most appetite.

BABY BEEF LIVER ....
Topped with crisp bacon.

BROILED PORK CHOPS ....
Two center cut chops chosen from tender young stock. Applesauce.

CHOPPED SIRLOIN STEAK ....
Choice ground sirloin.

Specialties of the House

PRIME RIB ....
Oven baked at low temperatures, creates a juicy cut that is unmatched.

SURF AND TURF ....
This 4 oz. of lobster meat combined with a 6 oz. tenderloin is a real crowd pleaser.

CHICKEN CORDON BLEU ....
A large chicken breast stuffed with spiced ham and Swiss cheese, and baked to a golden brown.

Fig. 13 Menu, Wright-Patterson Air Force Base.

the reason why their catering ability fits members' needs. This reminder of their offerings in catering has attracted substantial business.

Menus should have space for the addition of special dishes and events in dining. Menu clip-ons that direct attention to such events have added drawing power. The creative club menu must have all the variety of the local restaurant menu, and a special charm that the members will identify with to make the club "their club." The menu should have sufficient elegance so that members are proud to invite guests. Some clubs produce inexpensive reproductions of their menus and lists which can be mailed to homes.

With a controlled audience such parties as "Bon Voyage," "Monte Carlo Night," "Evening in Paris," "Man Who Came to Dinner," "80 Ways Around the World" are all possible. It is here that ingenuity displays itself. "The Candlelight Dinner," "Dinner with a Millionaire," "King Henry the Eighth," "Roman Orgy," "Masked Man," "Western Round-Up," "A Night in New Orleans," "The Las Vegas Buffet," are all possible themes. The trappings should be planned to complement the atmosphere.

One of the newest concepts is the gourmet dinner night. Normally there is one dinner a month. Menus and wine selections are published in advance. Reservations must be made a week prior. The set dinner may not be altered. One club reaches out for the finest chefs in the area and announces the name of the guest chef along with the menu.

CATERING AT THE CLUB   To keep the catering trade on base, the catering menu should be designed with art and copy that apply to the post. A "bright idea" book to assist in planning retirement parties or group cocktail parties is productive. A wine book that displays labels removes doubt from the customers' minds as to the professionalism of the establishment. After the catering menu and list is prepared it is a strong move to have individual pages reproduced so that prospective guests can have copies. A "Very Personally Yours" party folder spelling out all the essentials that will be provided enables the uncertain customer to make a quicker decision.

The catering menu must be simplified to avoid confusion. Indexing the menu with all types of situations enables the reader to turn directly to his or her areas of interest. It is also necessary to improvise. The catering service must emphasize the versatility of the organization in order to hold on to business. Small sketches incorporated into the menu provide a new look, and make the customer aware of the advantages of staying on base. The catering service must analyze what they have to offer that outside competition cannot.

Menus can be personalized for special occasions. For weddings there are many special possibilities: wine with the vintage year, the punch of the season, after-dinner drink in the bride and groom's favorite color, the Amaretto Love Cake, the layered cake in regimental colors, individual table cakes with coins stamped with the date.

The appeal of the catered party is the freedom it gives the host and hostess. If they have certain preferences, these should be honored. The creative catering service must be above competitive standards and have the ability to construct a reputation that stands on its own merits.

THE MILITARY BUFFET   Two haunting phrases on bases are "It looks the same," and "Everything tastes the same." The military buffet can be an exciting event, especially when themes provide the bases for menu changes. "The Hunt Breakfast," "Picnic Basket," "Gay Nineties Beer Party," "Toast of the Town," and "Roman Holiday," all enable the static buffet to offer new, more appealing food. The chosen wine in self-service bottles, the use of empty wine bottles with flowers, innovative desserts such as fruit in wine, fruit pie with cordial, ice cream with cordial pour, all enhance the meal.

One of the most successful adaptations was a "Cook Your Own" Buffet. Members had a choice of hamburgers, steaks or hot dogs. There was a huge open grill, surrounded by every type of trimming and dressing imaginable. Instead of wine the club had provided ten different types of domestic and imported beers and ale. Each guest was furnished a printed menu with suggestions for preparing various dishes as done in various parts of the world. The buffet turned into a beer tasting, with beers from Singapore, Germany, and France available. An everyday buffet was converted into a unique happening.

SUMMARY

The menus and wine lists offered by military clubs are taking on a bold new approach. The look of the menu, the naming of the items, the wine suggestions, and the decor are becoming more creative. It takes more ingenuity, more politics, and more profit concern to be a successful club manager and chef than in most civilian undertakings. Yet, the audience is there, and the closeness of relationships and the training capability are unique advantages. Today, the military menu is in many ways on a par with that of the civilian world.

PART II

WINE LISTS

5

THE WINE LIST— YESTERDAY AND TODAY

The wine lists of the late seventeenth century and the early eighteenth century were marvels of penmanship and calligraphy. Though gloriously embellished, reading was a problem. These wine lists appeared first in France, then England and Germany. There were two types of presentation books. The first was known as a captain's book, to be offered and handled only by the captain or maître d'. This was a collection of the actual labels representing the wines in their cellars, though not giving any explanation of the offerings. The second was their wine list, which could be offered to the customer by any employee, and it included every wine.

By the beginning of the nineteenth century, fine American restaurants were increasingly recognizing the eminence of French wines. There were virtually no American wines on these lists, a good assortment of German, and a limited number of Italian selections. The books were usually leather bound, with the name of the restaurant embossed on the front. Wines were not explained; the theory being anyone who could afford wine would be insulted by an explanation. Just prior to World War I, as America became increasingly brand conscious, establishments geared to wine began to give the customer books which displayed the wine label. These were dif-

65

ferent from the captains' books, in that the customers received their own copies. To this was later added information as to type, taste, aroma, color, and significance.

In today's restaurant world, wine is the new star on the horizon. The present wine boom has created a more knowledgeable wine customer. It has also resulted in an influx of newcomers who expect knowledgeable responses to their inquiries. The customers wish to avoid embarrassment in their lack of proper pronunciation and method of bottle handling. Therefore, they want the wine list and personnel to make them comfortable when ordering.

House wines have been a profit boon to most establishments. When the wine development programs started moving ahead, a void existed in restaurateurs' and patrons' knowledge of wine. The simplest way of entering the field was to offer a program of red, white, and rosé California wine. These wines were poured from larger containers and presented by the glass, carafe, and half carafe. In

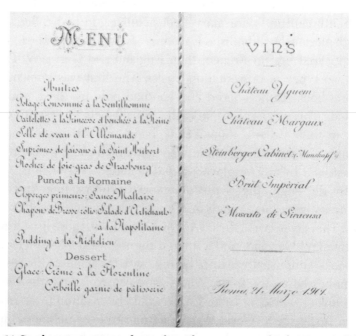

Fig. 14 Combination menu and wine list. Photo courtesy of Bohn-Bettoni Collection, University of Nevada, Las Vegas Library.

most cases, the shippers made available tent cards and various sales aids.

Suddenly there was a remarkable awakening at every restaurant level—an awareness that here was an interest that must be captured. The finer old line "carriage trade" restaurants had highly sophisticated lists of better French wines and a few German spatlese wines, but rarely an Italian, and only the most limited presentation of American wines.

At this point we saw the appearance of such menu phrases as "the wines of the house." Sunday brunches and buffets blossomed forth with free champagne. More and more restaurants wanted their champagne under their own label. The words, "Ask for our wine list" were seen with increasing frequency on menus. The wine world began to affect menu listings, popularizing dishes such as coq au vin, veal Marsala, tenderloin tips in red wine. Gourmet restaurants were ready and responded with dishes such as Cornish game hen in cognac, ham in Asti Spumante, turkey in champagne. One fine restaurant boasted that its cream pies were all flavored with imported liqueurs and topped with fresh fruit.

All this glory called for chefs and food and beverage directors possessing the knowledge to produce credible menu and wine lists.

PRESENTING THE WINE

Should the wine list be a separate presentation or combined with the menu? How lengthy should the wine list be? What proportion of domestic and imported wines should there be? Most important, what should the customer be told? The ultimate strategy that was developed throughout the food service industry in the early 1970s had to do with price levels. The expensive white tablecloth unit maintained a separate wine list, elaborately broken down by country and, in the case of California wines, by county. Some restaurants' lists showed maps of the areas, some drew on superior knowledge and incorporated legends, proverbs, and historical anecdotes. Each wine was carefully categorized on the wine list by vintage, variety, and what estate had bottled it. Each wine was described and labeled with its own bin number. Half bottles were stocked.

Customers have become appreciative of the romance of the bottle opening, the tasting, the presentation of the cork, the proper decanting, and pouring. One very famous Denver restaurant uses the opening page of their wine list to explain the routine and the reasons the stages were carried through. Another delivers the historic story of Dom Perignon and the various Catholic orders who have been associated with alcoholic beverages for centuries. Others have combined their wine lists with their menus, realizing that an overly elaborate presentation might frighten their guests. Some have gone a step further and added the phonetic pronunciation of the difficult French, German, and Italian wines.

Many of the finer restaurants nationwide have begun to employ European sommeliers. The sommelier emerged in the eighteenth century as a personality not to be tampered with. His wine recommendations were sought after. Arrogant and haughty, his decision was accepted with finality by the customer. He presented his wine list with dignity, and saw that the wine was properly stored and served in the customary manner.

Now the independent knowledgeable customer listens, but also displays his or her knowledge. He or she reads the list carefully. The moderately priced restaurant has had to meet the challenge of this type of customer in its selection and presentation of wines.

One of the newest innovations in wine service is the wine bar. There are several variations. In one, the taster is presented with a listing of the wines offered by the glass and can choose from a list of such dishes as quiche, shepherd pie, or various casseroles with a glass of wine at a fixed price. The wine-of-the-day is a bargain offer, selected from the better wines at a special, low price.

The artistry used in concocting these lists outdoes most menus. Wine labels are copied, history is given, and press clippings are used. Guest speakers are invited to give talks at the wine bars. Where the wine bar is set up in conjunction with a restaurant, the tasting is planned to tempt the customer into purchasing a full bottle with the meal.

THE WINE AND THE FOOD

Wine can sell the establishment. Last year I passed an appetizing-looking Italian self-service trattoria in St. Louis. The placemat was a photo of two baskets. The wine basket contained a popular Italian import; the breadbasket held a meatball and sausage sandwich. Alongside was a rough map of Italy showing where the wine was from, and a short explanation. This small family restaurant was using wine to establish the credibility of its Italian cookery.

In Monterey, California, a restaurant menu mentions that only authentic imported Sicilian marsala is used in its sauces. This made me respect their kitchen. A Hungarian restaurant in the Fairfax area of Los Angeles that had no wine list but displayed the labels of their great Hungarian wines and liqueurs let me know that here was a little bit of Hungary.

To walk into the cellar of an esteemed location in Miami and be literally swallowed up by thousands of bottles let me know that the food would be far above par, for the care of the wine cellar follows closely the care of the cuisine. To be questioned as to whether I preferred my fish to be prepared in Pouilly Fuisse or California chablis made me feel like an insider. On the other hand, to be given a fly-specked wine list with innumerable price changes or a laminated wine list cautions that here economy is king and leaves the diner uncomfortable.

There is an interrelationship between the menu and the wine list. The details of the menu influence the customers' expectations of the wine list. The number of chefs' offerings is an indication of the capacity of the cellar. The broad scope of appetizers and soups as well as the use of wine in the food preparation is another indication of what the customer can expect from the wine list.

The concern that the captain or server shows in assisting in the wine selection is an indication of the quality of the food itself. Aside from food quality and service, wine is the most potent factor in restaurant management today. For to talk of wine is to speak of many things, such as storage, service, and availability.

When the wine list lacks information, or when the restaurant is constantly out of certain types of wine, this might cause concern about the food. A stellar display of wines in a clean, visible vault or spotless cellar reflects the image of the kitchen. The bottle with a fresh flower, the rich leather in place of a shoddy paper, the elegance of the after-dinner menu are all symbolic of the meal. The restaurant that suggests that certain red wines need serious breathing time and that the guests order their wines in advance or when making reservations, has demonstrated that this same care and treatment will come in the guests' culinary pleasure. The restaurant that has gone through the turmoil, disappointments, and expense of preparing an extensive wine list must feel that the meals are a triumph for the deserving wine.

HISTORICAL BACKGROUND

Where and how did the wine revolution come about? How did it move from the most elegant of restaurants to the tables of coffee shops on Main Street, U.S.A.? What was the force that made supermarkets, liquor stores, and restaurants suddenly realize that wine was here?

If we look back through history we find that the fruit of the vine has always commanded the human imagination. The ancient Greeks referred to Italy as the land of wine. The Vikings gave the part of North America on which they landed the name Vineland or Vinland after the profusion of vines that were to be found there. The "viniculturi" of Caesar's legions were charged with the planting of vine cuttings along the marching routes, to sustain legions to come. These vines grew into the foundation of the European wine culture, changing character with the soil and climate. Napoleon's troops had their gigantic wine wagons and his servants carried his "canteen"— not for water but for his wine ration.

If we study the first wine lists that appeared in England and France during the early nineteenth century we find an abundance of red wines, with white and rosé a minority. By the start of the nineteenth century two practices appeared on the continent: Wine

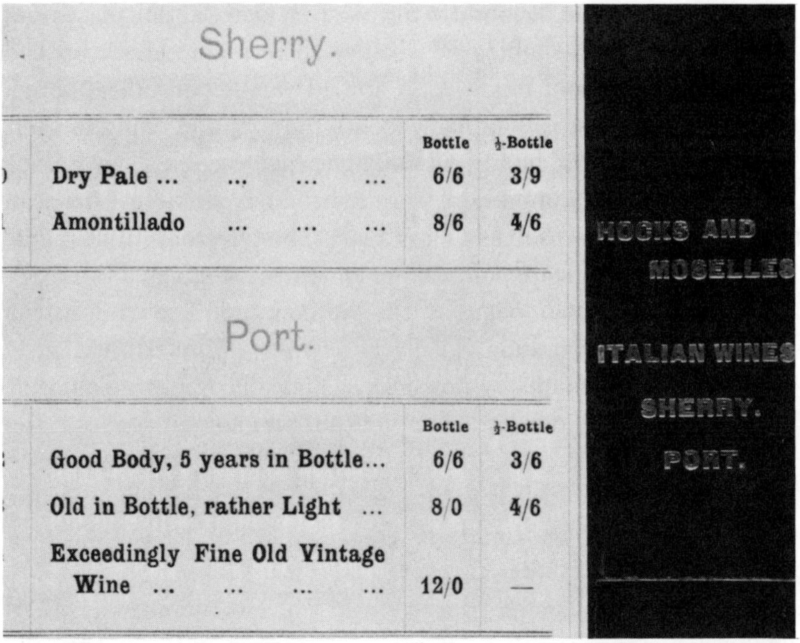

Sherry.		
	Bottle	**½-Bottle**
Dry Pale	6/6	3/9
Amontillado	8/6	4/6

Port.		
	Bottle	**½-Bottle**
Good Body, 5 years in Bottle...	6/6	3/6
Old in Bottle, rather Light ...	8/0	4/6
Exceedingly Fine Old Vintage Wine	12/0	—

HOCKS AND
MOSELLES

ITALIAN WINES

SHERRY.

PORT.

Fig. 15 Antique wine list. Photo courtesy of Bohn-Bettoni Collection, University of Nevada, Las Vegas Library.

lists were carefully annotated, each wine was carefully explained as to color, taste, and region. Lists recommended the proper wines for given food categories. The food was either illustrated or named on the left side of the carte with the names of wine on the right. Vintage years were stressed and many inns and eating places gave the capacity of their cellars. The special guest was often invited to a tour of the cellar where a particular favorite was opened. In America the sign of the cosmopolitan restaurant was to have the Carte de Vins in French. A step above the norm was the dining maestro who introduced the sommelier and the French serving manner. European, haughty, and domineering, his performance turned the opening of a. bottle into a mild extravaganza. In Europe, the restaurateurs of Italy, Germany, and France not only offered a wine list calculated to overwhelm the customer, but most had their own Vin de Jour, or house wine.

In the United States, by the early part of the twentieth century, wine listings were to be found at the most exclusive eating places and hotels. Only at the tables of wealthy society travelers who had learned to serve and enjoy wine abroad was it poured, although certain ethnic groups who had recently immigrated clung to their native wine drinking habits. Champagne had to come from France to be acceptable. Sommeliers were a rare bird; all were European and considered themselves a class apart. The Diamond Jim Bradys, movie stars, and certain political personalities established the superiority of French champagne in the public mind. The wine lists of the period consisted mainly of French wines, a limited number of German wines, practically no Italian wines and rarely a California wine. Much of the domestic wine output was homemade, and the foremost producers were the Italian immigrants who purchased their own grapes. Jewish groups enjoyed the sweet wines of the Concords on holy days and festivals.

In the United States prior to World War I, the wine list, backed up by a wine cellar, was offered in the most authoritative and elaborate restaurants and hotels, mainly located on the East coast, centered in New York. These wine lists were handsomely presented with great subtlety and finesse. In cities such as St. Louis, Chicago, and San Francisco the lists were marvels of scope. To have as many as one hundred and fifteen types of wine was not unusual. The presentation of the list was made by the maître d' or captain where a sommelier was not available.

One must recall that the menus and lists were works of pride. The foods were magnificently prepared and it was normal for the customer to eat a dinner of many courses. The merits of dieting were unknown and the eating and wine selection were carefully guided by the captains. The custom of toasting in champagne was prevalent, using anything less than champagne was a poor second. The restaurants vied with each other in offering the most magnificent first growths in a sequence of vintages.

The nouveaux riches were keenly aware that to arrive in proper society their homes must contain a proper cellar. When dining out it was considered a tribute to the guest to display elegance by having the proper wines served. The tour of the continent, traditional in high society prior to the war, was an introduction to fine wines and dining. The transatlantic liners of the United States, France, Germany, and Italy were a testimonial to the finest cuisine and wine selection. The decisive ability to order properly and with flair was indicative of having been abroad and an unmistakable part of status-building.

The private clubs of the period all carried extensive stocks of fine cognacs and sherries; vintage ports went along with the handsome Havana cigars that were a prime symbol of good taste. The concerned host at such a club was the sole recipient of the priced brochure. The entire mood created was a testimonial to the good taste and knowledge of the sponsor. While we salute the menu and wine facilities of the establishments of this time, they must be placed in perspective.

The eating places that formulated this presentation were few, as were the patrons who found them affordable. Beer was the beverage of the masses. The breweries were powerful and to a large extent controlled the location of the saloons and their finances. Competition was based on their free lunch bar and, to a limited extent, entertainment. Most had a special "Ladies Only" room, with a side street entrance. Whiskey was called for by name and this spirit dominated the hard liquor needs. Gin and vodka were commercially unknown to the consumer. Surprisingly these saloons also took great pride in their menus and the prices were calculated to fit the customers' needs. The brewers emerged with their own restaurants: among these were Busch, Berghoffs, and Schmidt. These restaurants were subsidized by the brewers for their commercial value in publicizing the name beer. In their praise is the fact that all had a fine wine list available.

When the Volstead Act passed, Prohibition arrived with an immediate degeneration of the fine restaurants that had served alcoholic beverages. The era of the speakeasy contributed little to the growth of premium wines. The period following the Prohibition era saw the emergence of a new type of restaurant—less ostentatious, more commercially oriented, more devoted to theme, decor, and food preparation. Wine lists were few and far between. In the period just prior to World War II there emerged two specific scenes. In restaurants with minimal menus geared to family budgets and commercial business, no alcohol was offered. The second category catered to young executives, and became famous for their culinary range and for presenting for the first time wine lists that were acceptably priced, introducing American wines from New York state and California. Some, such as the Brown Derby, Chasen's, Perrone's, Twenty-One, El Morocco, and the Pump Room, were gathering places for celebrities. Managements of these establishments introduced European chefs who were able to display their talents to an audience that was eager to taste and learn.

World War II exposed members of our armed forces to the wines and foods of the European countries. Military clubs sensed the changing times and showed more appreciation for customers' interest in wines. They served luscious foods and desserts foreign to American palates, which along with an emphasis on the pleasures of wine properly served, opened up a complete new awareness for their members.

THE WINE REVOLUTION

The names of Ernest and Julio Gallo should be enshrined in the heart of every individual in the wine industry. For, more than any other people or organization, they did the essential, head-on work in marketing that brought wine to the attention of the American public in the last thirty years. By producing wines that were priced fairly, well made, and well packaged, they made their products acceptable for sale on supermarket shelves, and accepted at tables.

Connoisseurs may find the taste qualities of such wines as Strawberry Hill and Boone's Farm Apple unacceptable. But it was wines such as these that indoctrinated the college market to wine, that fostered the entrance of Lambrusco, Liebfraumilch and many other popular imports. It has been said that the average wine drinker spends the first year with Gallo, and then experiments, and grows to be a wine lover. College students of the 1960s were not interested in hard liquor. Wine, however, offered a philosophy of history, geography, and affordability. Thus a pattern developed among those who received their first exposure to wine overseas,

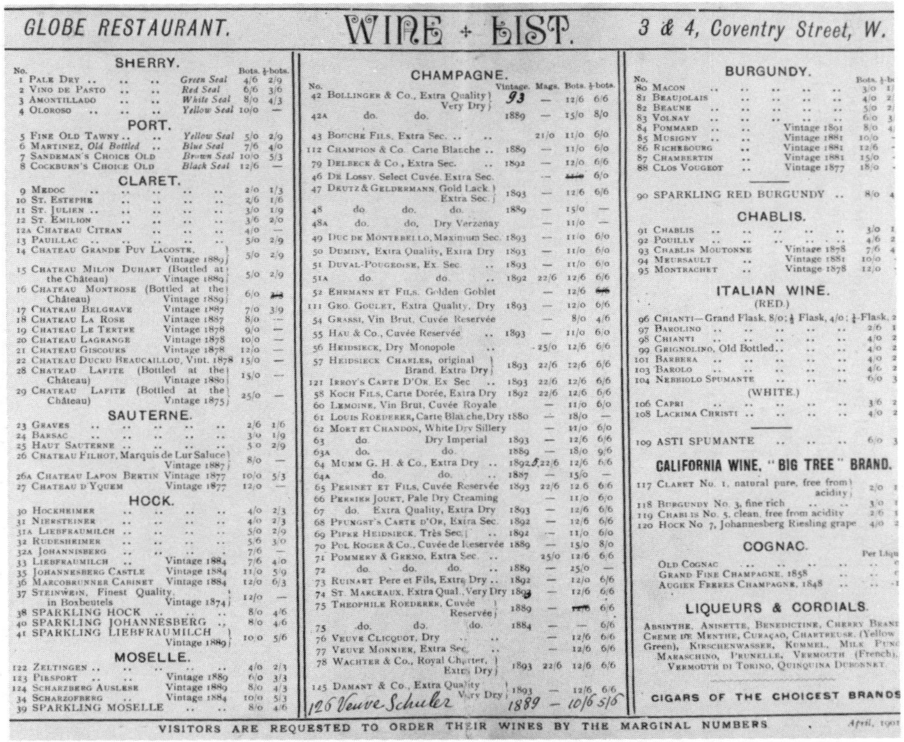

GLOBE RESTAURANT. WINE + LIST. 3 & 4, Coventry Street, W.

SHERRY.

No.			Bots.	½-bots.
1	Pale Dry	*Green Seal*	4/6	2/9
2	Vino de Pasto	*Red Seal*	6/6	3/6
3	Amontillado	*White Seal*	8/0	4/3
4	Oloroso	*Yellow Seal*	10/0	—

PORT.

5	Fine Old Tawny	*Yellow Seal*	5/0	2/9
6	Martinez, *Old Bottled*	*Blue Seal*	7/6	4/0
7	Sandeman's Choice Old	*Brown Seal*	10/0	5/3
8	Cockburn's Choice Old	*Black Seal*	12/6	—

CLARET.

9	Medoc		2/0	1/3
10	St. Estephe		2/6	1/6
11	St. Julien		3/0	1/9
12	St. Emilion		3/6	2/0
12A	Chateau Citran		4/0	—
13	Pauillac		5/0	2/9
14	Chateau Grande Puy Lacoste,	Vintage 1889	5/0	2/9
15	Chateau Milon Duhart (Bottled at the Château)	Vintage 1889	5/0	2/9
16	Chateau Montrose (Bottled at the Château)	Vintage 1889	6/0	[illegible]
17	Chateau Belgrave	Vintage 1887	7/0	3/9
18	Chateau La Rose	Vintage 1887	8/0	—
19	Chateau Le Tertre	Vintage 1878	9/0	—
20	Chateau Lagrange	Vintage 1878	10/0	—
21	Chateau Giscours	Vintage 1878	12/0	—
22	Chateau Ducru Beaucaillou, Vint. 1878		15/0	—
28	Chateau Lafite (Bottled at the Château)	Vintage 1880	15/0	—
29	Chateau Lafite (Bottled at the Château)	Vintage 1875	25/0	—

SAUTERNE.

23	Graves		2/6	1/6
24	Barsac		3/0	1/9
25	Haut Sauterne		5/0	2/9
26	Chateau Filhot, Marquis de Lur Saluce	Vintage 1887	8/0	—
26A	Chateau Lafon Bertin	Vintage 1877	10/0	5/3
27	Chateau d'Yquem	Vintage 1877	12/0	—

HOCK.

30	Hockheimer		4/0	2/3
31	Niersteiner		4/0	2/3
31A	Liebfraumilch		5/0	2/9
32	Rudesheimer		5/6	3/0
32A	Johannisberg		7/6	—
33	Liebfraumilch	Vintage 1884	7/6	4/0
35	Johannesberg Castle	Vintage 1884	11/0	5/9
36	Marcobrunner Cabinet	Vintage 1884	12/0	6/3
37	Steinwein, Finest Quality, in Boxbeutels	Vintage 1874	12/0	—
38	SPARKLING HOCK		8/0	4/6
40	SPARKLING JOHANNESBERG		8/0	4/6
41	SPARKLING LIEBFRAUMILCH	Vintage 1889	10/0	5/6

MOSELLE.

122	Zeltingen		4/0	2/3
123	Piesport	Vintage 1889	6/0	3/3
124	Scharzberg Auslese	Vintage 1889	8/0	4/3
34	Scharzofberg	Vintage 1884	10/0	5/3
39	SPARKLING MOSELLE		8/0	4/6

CHAMPAGNE.

No.		Vintage.	Mags.	Bots.	½-bots.
42	Bollinger & Co., Extra Quality Very Dry	93	—	12/6	6/6
42A	do. do.	1889	—	15/0	8/0
43	Bouche Fils, Extra Sec.		21/0	11/0	6/0
112	Champion & Co. Carte Blanche	1889	—	11/0	6/0
79	Delbeck & Co., Extra Sec.	1892	—	12/0	6/6
46	De Lossy. Select Cuvée. Extra Sec.		—	[illegible]	6/0
47	Deutz & Geldermann, Gold Lack Extra Sec.	1893	—	12/6	6/6
48	do. do. do.	1889	—	15/0	—
48A	do. do. Dry Verzenay		—	11/0	—
49	Duc de Montebello, Maximum Sec.	1893	—	11/0	6/0
50	Duminy, Extra Quality, Extra Dry	1893	—	11/0	6/0
51	Duval-Pougeoise, Ex. Sec	1893	—	11/0	6/0
51A	do. do.	1892	22/6	12/6	6/6
52	Ehrmann et Fils. Golden Goblet		—	12/6	[illegible]
111	Geo. Goulet, Extra Quality, Dry	1893	—	12/0	6/6
54	Grassi, Vin Brut, Cuvée Reservée		—	8/0	4/6
55	Hau & Co., Cuvée Reservée	1893	—	11/0	6/0
56	Heidsieck, Dry Monopole		25/0	12/6	6/6
57	Heidsieck Charles, original Brand, Extra Dry	1893	22/6	12/6	6/6
121	Irroy's Carte D'Or, Ex Sec	1893	22/6	12/6	6/6
58	Koch Fils, Carte Dorée, Extra Dry	1892	22/6	12/6	6/6
60	Lemoine, Vin Brut, Cuvée Royale		—	11/0	6/0
61	Louis Roederer, Carte Blanche, Dry	1880	—	18/0	—
62	Moet et Chandon, White Dry Sillery		—	11/0	6/0
63	do. Dry Imperial	1893	—	12/6	6/6
63A	do. do.	1889	—	18/0	9/6
64	Mumm G. H. & Co., Extra Dry	1892 5	22/6	12/6	6/6
64A	do. do.	1887	—	15/0	—
65	Perinet et Fils, Cuvée Reservée	1893	22/6	12/6	6/6
66	Perrier Jouet, Pale Dry Creaming		—	11/0	6/0
67	do. Extra Quality, Extra Dry	1893	—	12/6	6/6
68	Pfungst's Carte d'Or, Extra Sec.	1892	—	12/6	6/6
69	Piper Heidsieck, Très Sec	1892	—	11/0	6/0
70	Pol Roger & Co., Cuvée de Reservée	1889	—	15/0	8/0
71	Pommery & Greno, Extra Sec		25/0	12/6	6/6
72	do. do. do.	1889	—	25/0	—
73	Ruinart Pere et Fils, Extra Dry	1892	—	12/0	6/6
74	St. Marceaux, Extra Qual., Very Dry	189[illegible]	—	12/6	6/6
75	Theophile Roederer, Cuvée Reservée	1889	—	[illegible]	6/6
75	do. do. do.	1884	—	—	6/6
76	Veuve Clicquot, Dry		—	12/6	6/6
77	Veuve Monnier, Extra Sec		—	12/6	6/6
78	Wachter & Co., Royal Charter, Extra Dry	1893	22/6	12/6	6/6
125	Damant & Co., Extra Quality Very Dry	1893	—	12/6	6/6
126	Veuve Schuler	1889	—	10/6	5/6

BURGUNDY.

No.			Bots.	½-bots.
80	Macon		3/0	[illegible]
81	Beaujolais		4/0	[illegible]
82	Beaune		5/0	[illegible]
83	Volnay		6/0	[illegible]
84	Pommard	Vintage 1891	8/0	[illegible]
85	Musigny	Vintage 1881	10/0	—
86	Richebourg	Vintage 1881	12/6	—
87	Chambertin	Vintage 1881	15/0	—
88	Clos Vougeot	Vintage 1877	18/0	—
90	SPARKLING RED BURGUNDY		8/0	[illegible]

CHABLIS.

91	Chablis		3/0	[illegible]
92	Pouilly		4/6	[illegible]
93	Chablis Moutonne	Vintage 1878	7/6	[illegible]
94	Meursault	Vintage 1881	10/0	—
95	Montrachet	Vintage 1878	12/0	—

ITALIAN WINE.

(RED.)

96 Chianti—Grand Flask, 8/0; ½ Flask, 4/0; ¼-Flask, [illegible]

97	Barolino	2/6	[illegible]
98	Chianti	4/0	[illegible]
99	Grignolino, Old Bottled	4/0	[illegible]
101	Barbera	4/0	[illegible]
103	Barolo	4/6	[illegible]
104	Nebbiolo Spumante	6/0	[illegible]

(WHITE.)

106	Capri	3/6	[illegible]
108	Lackima Christi	4/0	[illegible]
109	ASTI SPUMANTE	6/0	[illegible]

CALIFORNIA WINE, "BIG TREE" BRAND.

117	Claret No. 1, natural pure, free from acidity	2/0	[illegible]
118	Burgundy No. 3, fine rich	3/0	[illegible]
119	Chablis No. 5, clean, free from acidity	2/6	[illegible]
120	Hock No 7, Johannesberg Riesling grape	4/0	[illegible]

COGNAC.

	Per Liqu[illegible]
Old Cognac	[illegible]
Grand Fine Champagne, 1858	[illegible]
Augier Freres Champagne, 1848	[illegible]

LIQUEURS & CORDIALS.

Absinthe, Anisette, Benedictine, Cherry Bran[illegible] Creme de Menthe, Curaçao, Chartreuse (Yellow [illegible] Green), Kirschenwasser, Kummel, Milk Pun[illegible] Maraschino, Prunelle, Vermouth (French), Vermouth di Torino, Quinquina Dubonnet.

CIGARS OF THE CHOICEST BRANDS

VISITORS ARE REQUESTED TO ORDER THEIR WINES BY THE MARGINAL NUMBERS. April, 1901

Fig. 16 Wine list, Globe Restaurant. Photo courtesy of Bohn-Bettoni Collection, University of Nevada, Las Vegas Library.

which combined with the interest in a better life of the graduating student body to give birth to the Wine Revolution.

The restaurant industry had a bull by the horns and nowhere to turn. Wine was being called for; it possessed enormous profit capability, and romance, and gave new excitement to a restaurant visit. The problems that existed were basically untrained personnel, lack of storage facilities, and lack of knowledge of proper presentation, skills in selling and serving, and in the greatest need of all, marketing. In this vital embryonic stage the wine wholesaler took on a new importance. The wholesaler was in a state of bewilderment, his personnel faced the same problems as the restaurants. There was no formal training, and it was certainly more expedient to sell a case of Scotch than become enmeshed in vintages, types, and availability and in the creation of wine lists.

The food and beverage directors of hotels accepted this new challenge. Those directors with European training took on special importance. Owners attempted to grapple with this vast trend developing around an entirely new type of knowledgeable customer, who many times was more informed than the server. Restaurants poured over trade publications, wine books, and columns. They received invitations from trade groups, wholesalers, and importers to attend tastings. The bottle or carafe on the table became a symbol of a new life-style, one that could alter the entire future of an enterprise. Some restaurant managers refused to accept the arrival of this exciting change, considering it a fad. Yet there were those responsible managers who, realizing the new potential, took full advantage of every authority on the subject. They researched wine habits, the history of the acceptance of wine and food, and utilizing all expertise available, they went to work. The experienced European restaurateurs had an instinct for the extent to which the role of wine would affect the diner's food tastes and planned drastic menu changes. Common intelligence laid down three precepts:

1. Written and spoken statements about wine must have credibility.
2. Wine pricing must be realistic in relationship to menu pricing and clientele.
3. Presentations must be informative and professional.

The aggressive merchant recognized the potential for growing profits that wine offered and developed cohesive programs including training of personnel, and attention to the environment in which wine is served. In former times, although the carriage trade restaurant had always maintained a wine list, the wines were not varied and were listed in a somber, unimaginative form, something like a bank statement. This leather-bound Captain's Book was rarely presented to the diner voluntarily, but only upon request. In it, wines were not explained, graphic design was not used to create an atmosphere. The customer was burdened with two volumes, a menu and a wine list. However, today's restaurateur recognizes the importance of a well-designed wine list.

There are a limited number of methods for planning a wine book or list. It may be created as a separate entity or be incorporated with the menu. My experience indicates that the customer gets more involved when ordering is simpler. The simpler appearance of the combined wine list and menu makes ordering easier for both customer and server. For many, ordering wine is far more important than ordering food. The clutter involved in looking at two lists is distracting, and therefore the skillful presentation of both elements simultaneously becomes impressive, and helpful. There are many roads to follow in making the wine listing complete. One route begins with a general heading, "To be enjoyed with red meats." Following this approach, wines are listed on the right side, and the foods suited to the wines in that group listed on the left. Conversely, on the same menu, the entrées each carry a recommended wine, with bin number. This double billboard makes the presentation with completeness and convenience.

The final word of the server or sommelier will tip the scale of selection. The wine list may be used to sell the menu. If an Italian restaurant breaks down its wines by region, it can list the speciality dishes of each area broken down the same way. Thus, if a Lambrusco is listed, from *Reggio Emilia*, it will follow that the golden *tortelli di erbetta* is the specialty dish.

When, to make the listing more memorable, we take the seasoned wine drinker into our confidence by stating which grapes the wine is blended from, we reassure the novice that he or she is not risking a wine budget on something of dubious quality. There are

White Wines

32   PINOT CHARDONNAY, Inglenook
        Dry, full-bodied, elegant
33   LANGHOF ZELLER SCHWARTZE KATZE
        Famed "Black Cat" Moselle Wine. Slight "spritz"
34   CHENIN BLANC, Inglenook
        Young, fresh, delicate, fruity and fragrant
35   LANGHOF PIESPORTER MICHELSBERG
        One of Germany's finest Moselle wines from the
        Piesporter region
36   FRENCH COLOMBARD, Sonoma Vineyards
        Pleasant bouquet, not too dry, excellent value
38   JOHANNISBERG RIESLING, Sonoma Vineyards
        Nesling
        Rich Spatlese taste, similar to German Moselle
40   MUSCADET, Marquis Goulaine
        Dry, fresh and clean
42   VOUVRAY, Monsieur Henri
        Semi-dry, light and fruity
44   POUILLY FUISSE, Mommessin
        Crisply dry, full-bodied, clean
46   SOAVE, Bolla
        Dry, light and elegant
48   BLUE NUN LIEBFRAUMILCH
        Light-bodied, fruity and luscious
50   DOMAINE DE CHEVAL BLANC
52   GRAVES, Dennis & Huppert
        Medium Dry, clean and crisp
54   CUVEE ST. PIERRE, Mommessin
55   BARON DE LUZE, BORDEAUX

Champagnes & Sparkling Wines

56   DOM PERIGNON, Moet & Chandon
        The world's premier champagne
58   PIPER HEIDSIECK N.V.
60   MARTINI & ROSSI ASTI SPUMANTE
62   CHAMPAGNE BRUT, Sonoma Vineyards
64   CHAMPAGNE BRUT, Taylor New York State
        Classic, distinguished, very dry
66   SPRITZEN GERMAN SPARKLING WINE
67   HENRI PIPER JULI BRUT SPARKLING WINE FRANCE
        From Piper Heidseick
        A sparkling wine, delicious taste, romantic bouquet
68   GOLD SEAL N.Y. STATE BLANC DES BLANCS

Our World of Red Wines
Recommended with steaks, roasts and red meats

Our Selection of White Wines
Ideal with poultry, seafood and salads

Light and Brite Rose Wines
Veal, lamb and fruits

The Finishing Touch
We recommend the COINTREAU GLOW served on warmer at your table. A dash of Brandy into
which we pour a lavish serving of Cointreau. Slowly warmed at your table to bring
out the bouquet. Served with Orange wedge. Unforgettable.

Fig. 17 Wine list, The Terrace Room.

endless stories of customers ordering wine, claiming it's been falsely represented, and provoking arguments—proving that a little knowledge is dangerous. The wine customer who sent back a bottle of beautiful *Riserva Chianti*, loudly proclaiming "real" Chianti arrived in a straw basket, is not as bad as the "connoisseur" of German wine who returned a bottle of Liebfraumilch, claiming the restaurant must be covering up a bad wine because the glass was brown.

To a wine lover the magic world of wine is imaginative, romantic, and adventuresome. Then why not propose the structuring of a wine list that has these fantasy elements? There are endless quotations and proverbs having to do with wine. The use of these adages will serve to embellish the starkness of the program and provide conversation, which indeed is the soul of wine selling technique. A true wine customer is influenced as much by the atmosphere of the brochure as by the actual wines, for the wines may be taken for granted, but the side comments act as a testimonial to the concern of management.

There is a restaurant in Boston, for example, which maintains a superb cellar. Its cobwebs are never touched, the drippings of candles that have been burned there still remain. Certainly these trappings do not add to the wines' taste, but customers insist on having a bottle when in this atmosphere.

To position a restaurant for a given market, it may be necessary to expand current services. Restaurant owners have set new goals. They open early on Sunday, or stay open later on a given weekday evening and give private tastings. Menus are printed with greater readability, illustrations are thought out. Wines are listed with explanations, and pronunciations, described in words that display knowledge but protect the establishment from embarrassment. The lists are of a manageable size, on paper that will stand up, in colors that belong with the decor, in designs that are individual and enhance the image of the restaurant.

Staffs increasingly have their own tasting and training program, which, coordinated with the presentations, enable the server to be familiar with wine and have the right answers. The modern manager maintains a file of his competitors' menus and wine lists. By updating his reading he becomes alert to changing wine tastes.

Many customers have become interested in ordering wine with lunch. The easy way to do this has often been to order the house wine, by the glass or half carafe. Because of this demand, a new element suddenly appeared on tables: the half-bottle list. This was a mini listing of a few champagnes or sparkling wines followed by about eight other wines. The half bottle was perfect for two at lunch, but again the customer has wanted an explanation and the full treatment. The mini list is here and growing as an addition to regular business.

6

PLANNING THE INDIVIDUAL WINE LIST

To those dedicated to focusing the attention of their clientele solely on wines there are certain no-nonsense basics.

The bin number should be in large type, or if possible, in a second color, directly alongside the wine. This eliminates the necessity of pronunciation, and simplifies ordering for both the server and customer.

The most common method of listing wines is by group, such as champagne and sparkling, white, red, and rosé. The customer may turn quickly and efficiently to the group which interests him or her. The alternative is grouping by country and type. If this familiar method is used, it follows that each nation should be broken down by region. A caption might read, "The Historic White Wines of Germany," followed by, "The Historic Rhine Wines" and "The Fabled Moselles." The advantage of this procedure is that it enables the restaurant to display the integrity and completeness of its offerings. Under this system, the wines of California would be listed by county, and New York wines by region.

One of the greatest wine lists in the country is presented by a nationally known restaurant in Florida. Here, the wines of each nation are presented separately, and each wine has its vintage carefully annotated. A great hotel in Atlanta illustrates each region alongside the wines and stars the wine of the region. At the start of this wine list a typical label is illustrated and the reader is instructed on the significance of each statement on the label. When the bottle is presented the purchaser has a finer appreciation of the meaning of the wine as stated on the label.

The owner of one San Francisco restaurant places his initials alongside specific wines. This form of endorsement personalizes the selection of the house. The wine list states that no wine appears until the owner and staff have personally made a tasting.

EXPLAINING THE WINE

If the creator of the list wants to use color as the guideline, then the list could be captioned "Our World of Red Wines," followed by a comment that red wines are best suited to red meats, such as beef. Below this, wines could be broken down into subcategories: the wines of California, the wines of France, etc. There are those who believe this is overly repetitive. Not true! It is an effective manner of supplying complete information on each page. As a rule of thumb, if the wine list is brief, then the color category is sufficient. If the list is extensive, it follows that the clientele is wine-oriented and the more in-depth breakdown is appropriate, since for this type of operation the country or county of origin is of extreme importance to the customer.

The creative wine list regards the customer with respect. He or she is reading the wine list out of interest. The customer deserves complete information, stated simply, definitely, and believably. The functional wine list should be so complete that no questions are necessary.

Regarding wine, nothing is obvious. The explanatory listing provides a guideline with known facts, such as vintage year, bottling estate, vineyard, and grape characteristics. Carried further, it could include information on non-vintage wines, phonetic pronunciation, one-line explanations of taste, aftertaste, body, dryness, and color. The essential purpose of the wine list is to present the total capacity

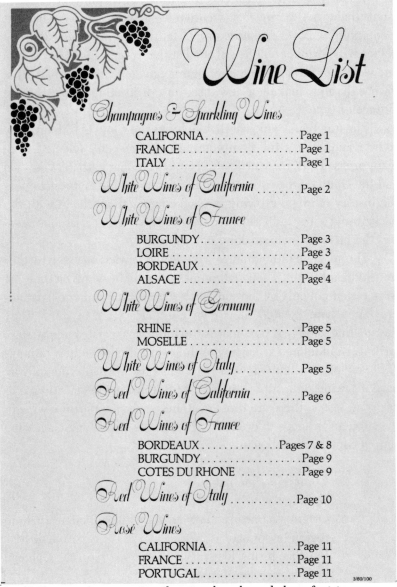

Fig. 18 This wine list categorizes the wines by color and place of origin.

of the collection in the simplest, most functional, and complete manner. Structure the reading so that customers may locate their area of interest in the least possible time. Furnishing brief statements that give the wine facts facilitates selection. The wine list that is complete removes embarrassment, and makes ordering easy. The novice wine drinker will resent the list that reveals his or her lack of knowledge in pronouncing a foreign language. The informed wine lover will enjoy making a new discovery or locating an old favorite vintage or type.

The functional wine list that includes the wines of California by county may offer a full complement of Cabernets, selected from many areas. Thus the wine lover becomes familiar with the vineyard and the county. One eating place in Sacramento tells its customers the history of grape growing in each county, then fills in with the background of the individual vineyards. The reading is fascinating— it is the history of winemaking in a capsule.

The surge to individualize wine lists is carried one step further by a hotel in Boston. Their statement is that all the wines on their list were tasted not only by the staff but a significant number of customers. They have created their own grading system in stars. They caution that wine is as personal as the individual palate and the stars are only a guideline. According to their system, the highest rating is **** and obviously the lowest is *. This raises the question of why have a * wine on a superb wine list. Because wine selection is as varied as tastes, there are those customers who support the wine in question and choose to order it. The listings describing each wine should contain the following:

1. Complete wine name.
2. Brand or vineyard.
3. Origin—name of country or state is insufficient. Include region or county.
4. Bottling terms like private reserve, reserve, Château bottled, are significant.
5. Vintage—if specific year is available list it. If a supply problem exists and you can't, then the letter "V" or word Vintage should appear.
6. Other information on the calibre of the wine: aged in

cask, naturally fermented, fermented in the bottle.

7. Clarification of the use of the word "champagne" is necessary in listings of sparkling wines and champagnes. With the surging popularity of Blanc de Blancs, sparkling wines, and other selections in this category, this will avoid confusion. Clarification is worthwhile in the case of "Spumante" versus Asti Spumante as well. The same is true of The Deutches Sekt of Germany. One very fine New York dining room's list runs a paragraph which explains the protective nomenclature of "champagne."

8. The terminology that applies to these wines will be appreciated by the studious reader: Brut, Extra brut (extra dry), Sec, Demi-sec, and Doux. Café des Deux Mâgots, a renowned Parisian café, presents guests ordering champagne with a brochure containing history, and information on production methods, grapes, storage and serving of the wine.

9. Recommended with listings of important Châteaux is their order of growth, First, Second, etc. The emphasis on the standards adds immeasurably to a list. Many restaurants announce that vintage charts for France, California, Italy, and Germany are available.

10. Color—"white" is a misnomer. You can describe wine as straw, pale gold, and gold. The reds are garnet, ruby, pomegranate, crimson, purple red, scarlet, rosé, pink-light red, pale red, and pink. The words, brilliant, dull, and clear clarify meaning.

11. Details on the "body" of the wine: well rounded, fine consistency, lacks firmness, tart, fruity, soft, mellow, and nutty.

12. Statements on taste are most complicated. The applied words or phrasings must place the wine in the proper context. Well balanced, rough, hard, sound, are all words describing taste. Write about the wine's nature and characteristic qualities using words and phrases like dry, semi-dry, absence of sweetness, opposite of sour.

13. Descriptions and definition of the "nose" of the wine. This is the total fragrance as apart from "bouquet," which is the total smell from fermentation and aging. The "aroma" originates from the grapes. Discuss all three on your wine list.

14. Aftertaste is another area important to the more appreciative wine taster. Aftertaste is the culmination of wine pleasure. On a San Francisco pier, a nationally recognized fish restaurant states, "Our Zuppa di Pesce (fish soup) will make love to your palate. Our Verdicchio will leave it tingling." The enthusiast enjoys every nuance of wine selection. By commenting on aftertaste you have completed the appraisal.

Conscious of the interest in wines, an aware restaurateur might combine the wine list with the menu, thereby stimulating wine sales, avoiding cluttering the table with two separate lists, and, incidentally, enabling the customer to make selections with greater ease. The food server saves time and can perform more rapidly and with more assurance. Placing the name of the recommended wine under the entrée lends credibility to the dish and the wine. Placing the name of the wine alongside or beneath the dish removes the possibility of embarrassment for the customer who may be just getting to know wine.

Knowing the extent of the clientele's education in wine is a must. Technical words and phrases that appeal to the wine lover may injure the pride of the tyro. Here are some specific examples: Wine lists may use the initials that designate the quality of a wine—The AC or *Appellation Controllée* of France, the DOC or *Denominazione di Origine Controllata* of Italy, QBA or *Qualitatswein* and *Qualitatsweinmit Predikat* of Germany. All these symbolize authenticity and government control, and represent the credibility of the list and the cellar. However, the story is told of an engineer who saw AC after a French wine and DOC following an Italian, remarked he had never known about the use of electricity in wine making. Many wine lists use the letters and explain their significance to avoid this confusion.

One of the most unique wine lists I have ever seen was in Mexico City. Upon being seated we were given a handsomely embossed book, captioned, The Wine Words of El Portal: Our Wine Library. A departure from normal lists, this one contained no breakdown by type, but listed all wines alphabetically. The book was indexed by dictionary-style tabs, with, for example: all Châteaux under "C" and Brunello di Montelcino under "M." Alongside each wine were the control letters, and under "S" for symbols was a comprehensive explanation of each symbol.

The creator of the list may wish to explain the original importance of vintage history. First applied in the seventeenth century when the production of bottles and corks made the storage of wine possible, the heritage has been kept as a kind of consumer protection.

In Northern California it is not uncommon to find the trade words, "varietal" or "generic" on lists. Some believe that the blended wines should be so listed. To be informative on German wines is a mouth-filling journey. Numbers of lists now explain the words, Kabinett, Spatlese, and Auslese. Explanation of the price differential of vintage plus type makes a world of difference and is a dispute preventative. A Piesporter Goldtropchen Spatlese '76 will obviously command a substantially higher price than a Piesporter QBA '79. The greater the extent of details supplied, the simpler and more precise the ordering process becomes.

The obvious question to ask is, where does it end? How much information is enough? You must know your customers and what prompts the bottle sale. The expensive restaurant may feel that its clientele does not need the phonetic spelling but that the vintage year and vineyard are necessary and that the control symbols must be utilized. All that need be stated will be accomplished in two lines, no need for more space. The words of the wine list are indicative of the concern for the guest and also helpful for the server. Let the facts be so stated as to remove doubt and confusion. There must be an alertness to individual needs. The list should not be an ego trip but a useful, positive arrangement to furnish that material that makes wine ordering a successful, enjoyable exercise.

THE BIN AND THE BIN NUMBER   The number placed alongside the individual wine listing is referred to as the bin number. The
strategic importance of this number is ignored and misunderstood
by too large a segment of the dining industry. Use of this one symbol
can remove any degree of misunderstanding on the part of the guest
and the server.

Bin number is a term that historically goes back to the English
club. Each member's tobacco, cigars, and wines were "binned" on
an individual basis and numbered. Nowadays, bin numbers are used
in many establishments to designate each wine on the list. Their
essential purpose is to remove the neccessity of enunciating the
many unfamiliar names, expressions, and terms found in imported
wines. This removes embarrassment from both the guest and the
server.

An airport restaurant in upper New York state has the wine
vault completely enclosed in glass. Diamond-shaped bins are
formed by criss-crossed beams. Each bin carries a plaque with the
number and wine name. This same display is pictured on the outside
of the wine list, the bins are numbered and named as on the display.
A customer has the advantage of seeing the wine selection, then
referring to the information given on the list.

A very elegant restaurant in St. Petersburg, Florida, has a
masterful display of all their wines on a racked display, completely
exposed. Individual cards are posted beneath each wine. The card
gives full details of the bottle, and the bin number is printed in color.
Should the guest be enthusiastic about the wine a duplicate bottle is
available.

A private country club that maintains a wine book of labels
illustrates another approach. Their book is kept on a podium-type
table, and is beautifully leather bound. Below each label are listed
the vintages available and the bin number.

The bin number deserves aesthetic treatment on the wine list.
It should be large, well spaced and immediately recognizable. This
may be done through many interesting techniques. A hotel in
Honolulu places the number in the center of a drawing of a wine
cask. An establishment in Phoenix, Arizona insets the number in
geometric squares and triangles with varied colors. The blue back-

The Wines of Our House

Red Wine

Bin No		Bottle	Half Bottle
1.	CABERNET SAUVIGNON Leme Freres (California) Well rounded body, flavorful, fruity bouquet.	4.50	.....
2.	ZINFANDEL Leme Freres (California) Full Bodied and fruity with distinct "berry" flavor.	3.75	.....
3.	DRY LAMBRUSCO (cork) Giacobazzi (Italy) Refreshing, lively wine with the "frizante" touch.	5.50	3.25
4.	SUPERIOR ROUGE Rene DuBarry (France) Bordeaux regional wine, characteristic taste and bouquet.	4.75	.....
5.	CLARET Juan Hernandez (Spain) Ruby red, dry palate, soft vineyard aroma.	4.50	.....

Rosé Wine

Bin No		Bottle	Half Bottle
21.	ROSÉ Mateus (Portugal) Medium sweet, light and bright.	8.50	.....
22.	ROSATO Giacobazzi (Italy) Alive with flavor, semi-dry, mellow and refreshing.	5.50	3.25
23.	SUPERIOR ROSÉ Rene DuBarry (France) Subdued "grapey" taste, fine bouquet, Bordeaux regional.	4.75	.....

Leme Freres House Wine

LEME FRERES CALIFORNIA SELECTION

		Glass	Half Liter 16 oz.	Full Liter 33 oz.
41.	VINE ROSE	.85	2.25	3.75
42.	CHABLIS	.85	2.25	3.75
43.	BURGUNDY	.85	2.25	3.75
44.	Available in half-bottles (12 oz.) 1.75			

White Wine

Bin No		Bottle	Half Bottle
11.	FRENCH COLUMBARD Leme Freres (California) Light and fruity, crisp and clean.	4.25	.....
12.	CHENIN BLANC Leme Freres (California) Fresh and attractive, mild sweetness.	4.00	.....
13.	BIANCO Giacobazzi (Italy) Vivacious, semi-dry, light and bouncy.	5.50	3.25
14.	SOAVE Barberini (Italy) Famed soft wine of Verona, gold, excellent with fish and fowl.	5.50	3.25
15.	LIEBFRAUMILCH Kronenwein (Germany) Most popular Rhine wine, mild, fruity and semi-dry.	5.00	.....
16.	SUPERIOR BLANC Rene DuBarry (France) Typical dry taste of Bordeaux region, flowery bouquet.	4.75	.....
17.	PIEPORTER GOLDTROPFCHEN Kronenwein (Germany) Gentle golden wine, soft and delicate, semi-dry.	6.50	.....

Sparkling Wine

Bin No		Bottle	Half Bottle
31.	ASTI SPUMANTE Barberini (Italy) Great Italian sparkling wine, semi-dry, full of life.	10.00	.....
32.	CHATEAU MONOPOLE CHAMPAGNE Full champagne flavor and sparkle, the celebration wine.	6.25	.....
33.	CHATEAU MONOPOLE SPLITS	1.75	.....

Cordially yours—from our liqueur and cordial orchards. Your choice 1.25

Imported French Cognac 2.50

Fig. 19 This wine list uses bin numbers as well as wine names.

ground indicates an import, a red background, domestic wine. Printing the numbers in a second color highlights their importance.

Going back to the original meaning of bin numbers, the restaurant Twenty-One in New York offers regulars a bin of their own. Another New York restaurant, Windows on the World offers this service and also purchases the wines for their diners. A world-recognized Greek shipping magnate, when entertaining, distributes his private wine list, hand lettered, with his comments. A picture of Bacchus is placed alongside each wine and Roman numerals state the bin number.

However, the fact is that few designers employ thought in making the numerals work for them—as they can. A rare instance is a restaurant in Bordeaux. On their wine list is a beautifully illustrated panel, entwined with grapevines, with the numbers set in individual frames in capital Caslon letters. The panel bleeds off the page giving it a striking resemblance to a bookmark, and the impact of the number is enhanced. If we are to sell wine, to live with wine, and to afford the pleasure of wine, then the satisfaction and ease of reading a wine list must be part of this fulfillment.

DESIGN

While dining out, the wife of our host remarked, "We'll never get dinner served, my husband gets more pleasure out of reading a wine list than most men do from a great novel." Simple, well-spaced, with easy-to-read type, a well-documented wine list can be entertaining, informative, and stimulating.

No two wine listings should run together. Each listing must stand apart. There should be a minimum of two lines of space between entries. To look at a list of one hundred wines that is not properly spaced is to look upon a massive "blurb." One fashionable restaurant sets parentheses around each wine. This tends to make the individual wine more important, setting it apart from the total list.

No law states that wine lists must be precisely columnar. There are many avenues of departure. In one listing I saw recently, the type follows a half-circle shape and runs around a magnificent re-production of an old steel etching of a vineyard scene. Another approach could be a series of rectangles, in which each type of wine—red, white, rosé, and sparkling—is listed in separated blocks. These small variants can make the presentation unique. Typefaces have individual character and so can be chosen to tie in with the general decor. Certain faces are easy to read; others, while pleasing the creative ego, may cause eyestrain when the lights are dim. An Italian ristorante would not feel comfortable with an Old English type, and the restaurant seeking a comprehensive image would not be in tune with a Roman Caslon. Proofs of a menu or wine list should be read in the light of the restaurant and not in a well-lit office.

To reinforce the customers' memories, the logotype of the eating place should be used wherever possible. For example, the overall management of a group of restaurants located in the same area in downtown Los Angeles found it necessary to design indi-vidual logos for each establishment. The lettering and visual ele-ments of each menu reflect the type of food served. For lunch, the self-service counter offers six-ounce bottles of wine. On each is Kleen-Sticked a small reminder, "Wine Time," with the counter's emblem. The individuality is expressed not only in the logo but the color scheme as well.

Where the wine list and the menu are separate, the design and character should be similar, but the background color should vary. The simplification of the brochure is important not only to the client but to the server as well. With the high turnover of restaurant personnel, the ability to easily read the menu and locate items on it makes the service more dignified.

7

SERVING THE WINE

For centuries, tavern keepers of Europe, or the hostelries of Colonial times served the guest from casks of wine. In the main these were generic, inexpensive wines and were often served free or included with the meal price. In New England there was "mulled" wine, cider, and local grape and berry wines. In England beer and ale were most popular beverage. The wine was imported in casks from France.

In France and Italy the owner poured his own wine selection. These were decanted from the cask to a carafe which contained approximately one liter. The French proprietor, as he is today, was extremely proud of his wine choice. Today there are many restaurants that have their wine carry a label that identifies the wine as being of their restaurant or brasserie. These wines are served from the bottle. In the United States house wines are poured either from mechanically cooled, artificial barrels or from three- and four-liter containers into the serving carafe. With the invention of the self-contained three- and five-liter pouring containers that are made with their own spouts, carafe serving became simpler and less expensive.

HOUSE WINES

There is a division of opinion whether to identify the house wine. As these are mainly "jug" wines, the consumer rarely sees the vineyard name. To protect the owner's option of changing brands, many feel it is better to simply call the wine "Our House Wine." Others feel that giving the name of a classical vineyard assures the buyer that the wine is of good quality. The budget-conscious restaurant catering to families, students, and low cost meetings finds that jug wine offers the most adaptable pricing. Contrary to popular opinion many of these wines are well made and sound. The public has discovered their inherent value and sales of large sizes are increasing. House wine by the carafe can be merchandised in many ways.

Offering the house wine on the menu and wine list is one obvious method of presentation. As always, clever departures from the obvious will catch a customer's eye. One establishment keeps a barrel near the door with the sign, "This is the barrel our wines were aged in." One bar hangs empty three-liter bottles for decoration. Designing a list of house wines and pasting this on an empty bottle, which is then placed on the table, is an excellent reminder. A memorable table tent pictured the two owners of the bar tasting wine while surrounded by hundreds of bottles. The caption on the tent stated: "Only if it's good enough for us do we serve it to you." Another clever presentation was a bottle hanger in the form of a grape cluster with the message, "The next best thing to drinking in a vineyard is our wine from the jug."

While most of the vineyards supply sellers with attractive and colorful table tents, it is the ingenious owner who provides the personal touch. One clever table tent is in the shape of a wine basket and sits on the table with the consoling message, "We don't make our own—but we pick it." Another tent, die cut in the form of a half-filled wine glass, carries these words, "Picture the pleasure that a glass of our house wine would give." A chain of steak houses has a bottle hanger stamped in gold that reads, "Our wine of the month." Attached to their menu is a booklet that explains their house wine policy. They change the wine each month and ask for customer comments. Wine receiving the most favorable comments is brought back. On each carafe of wine the name of the brand is presented and an accompanying booklet tells the wine's background and gives a map of the area wherein the grapes are grown. They have established their restaurant as a tasting ground where wine drinking will be fun.

Along with its policy of offering as much free wine as the customer desires, one Italian restaurant uses a menu clip-on that provides the customer with the information that wine increases the appetite, makes food more enjoyable, and aids the digestion. The clip-on is done in a cartoon style. A slap at snob wine appeal is the hanger that reads, "If you can say *red, white,* or *rosé,* we'll take your wine order." The decoration is a sommelier's chain and tasting cup. Possibly the greatest impulse wine seller is the clip-on. By using a contrasting color and clever art, attention is quickly drawn to the inexpensive pleasure of the house wine.

Recently a most sophisticated new twist is being used: the "Vin de Jour" or wine of the day. This is not a jug wine, rather it is a superior wine offered at very near cost to give the patron the opportunity of enjoying a better wine. The merchandising philosophy is that, given the opportunity of tasting better wines, ultimately customers will turn to better wines with their dinners. In Philadelphia, the Avant Garde restaurant publishes a Vin de Jour wine schedule. The layout is similar to a football schedule sheet. The wine, the date, and the wondrous comments of the owner pertaining to the wine are given. The proprietor reports that many customers use the back of the card for tasting notes, and that he has had to reshape the card to fit into a wallet. As a direct result of this program his better wine sales have increased as have his carafe sales.

There are establishments that concentrate on wine by the glass. One lunchtime I walked into a bar and was greeted with a two-sided table tent which read "The Best of Both Wine Worlds." On one side was the story of their California house wine, the other their regional French wine. Each label was centered on the card. An associate sent me an attractive folder. The outside read, "The wines of our house are our house wines." Inside was displayed an Italian,

French, German, and California wine, with the subheading, "We believe our wine-loving friends deserve a choice."

For customers who like to experiment with new wines, ordering by the glass or by the carafe is a chance to experience some new tastes. Possibly one of the strongest ploys was a menu clip-on of a hotel that called out, "If you dine here seven days in a row, we will offer a distinctly different carafe wine on each visit." The development of a wine customer begins with carafes. He moves cautiously and budget-wise from the carafe to the bottle. The more variable the wine carafe program, the greater exposure the customer gets to the joys of wine.

The Six-Ounce Bottle

There was a time when the six-ounce bottle was the sole angel of the airlines. Now this size is appearing in delis, buffets, cafeterias, industrial feeding areas, stadiums and the military. These bottles, immersed in ice, need no service. Screw-cap lids make opening simple, and an extra sale is made. Resorts have discovered that by adding their logo to the bottle, the bottle becomes a charming and unusual souvenir. Airline terminal establishments have effectively used this size for the rushed traveler who enjoys wine. At one terminal there is a menu clip-on that reads, "Just enough time for wine time."

The most rewarding sales area is the luncheon menu. A cafeteria states, "One of life's little luxuries—our six-ounce minis." Unbeatable for buffets, the bottle is taken from the ice and charged on the tray. A bottle hanger states: "Try our handy size minis—just enough!" One industrial cafeteria sparks sales with this table tent: "Spark up your afternoon with our little wine wonders." There is no question that in military clubs this size has taken a hold.

While there are severe legal problems, vending machine producers are currently working on dispensing equipment that will open new markets. Restaurants nationally that pack lunches have discovered the magic of the six-ounce size. One hotel offers a picnic basket with deli, cheese, fruit, and French bread plus a mini bottle. This bottle, says one manager, "is the charmer." In the selling of wine, with its universal appeal in today's dining world, there appears to be a market for each size. Like all things that involve merchandis-

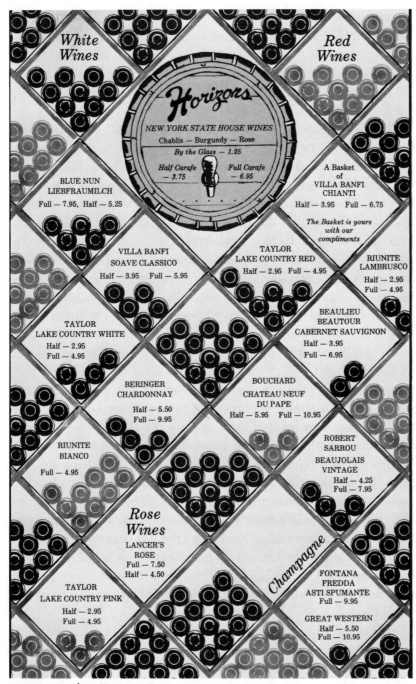

Fig. 20 Wine list, Horizons Restaurant.

ing and presentation, it is the adaptive program that will flourish.
Wine should never be a crutch, it must be a plus.

THE WINE BAR

Travel in Paris and you will come upon small intimate shops
that offer a variety of fine wines by the glass, along with sausage,
cheese, and sandwiches. The pride of the owner in his wine selection is highly personal. His choice of cheeses meshes with the wine
he offers. There is always a counter and a limited number of tables.
The owner has visited the vineyards and is known to deal directly
with the vineyards. Here in a relatively short time one may enjoy a
fine glass of wine and a snack at a modest price. These wine bars
open early and close late. Across the Channel in London the wine
bar has the atmosphere of a private club. The dishes offered are
quiche, shepherd's pie, cold roast beef and salads. The list of wines
in both cases is presented in a similar manner, on a handwritten list
or in chalk on a blackboard. In both instances the wines are offered
by the glass and change constantly. The English wine bar is just
beginning to offer California wines. For a full lunch with wine, these
wine bars are becoming very popular. San Francisco boasts of one of
the first wine bars opened, combining a bar with a wine shop for
retail sales. Another such wine bar and retail store is to be found in
Marina del Rey. Currently many hotels are redecorating unused
areas to look like wine cellars with tasting benches and stalls. One
restaurant that is converting a cocktail lounge to a wine bar has the
walls filled with enlargements of famed wine labels. The ledges are
loaded with bottles of wine. Each week the owner prepares a tasting
critique which is distributed to his clientele. A wine bar newly
opened in New Orleans has a customer tasting panel. The results of
their findings are published for customers' use. Wines that meet the
panel's approval are placed on the list.

That the wine bar is here and growing is a fact. That the wine
bar with the addition of a wine shop will prove its merit remains to be
seen. It is an area where creativity in atmosphere and presentation
will be fundamental to its success.

SPECIALIZED WINE LISTS

The Mini-Wine Card   The mini-wine card is a list of not more than eight wines, all offered in half bottles. Usually there is one champagne and the rest are divided between imports and domestics. There have been some clever developments on this theme. "Just enough time to get romance started." "Don't just eat—dine, with a half bottle of wine." One restaurant located outside of Las Vegas places a different half bottle with label on each table when setting up for lunch. In each bottle is a fresh rose.

Since the appearance of these half bottles and the mini list, the half-bottle sales have tripled. One cut-out bottle hanger is in the shape of a clock, and reads "There are twelve ounces in our half bottles—they make each moment enjoyable." Rarely have I seen a mini-list that does not have a cute twist. One states, "Not enough— we always have a second." "We'll make your luncheon sparkle with our half bottles of California Champagne." One is partially folded over, and the border reads, "Our little bottles are mighty good."

Some restaurateurs have turned from an actual list to placing their offerings on table tents and menu clip-ons. A large number of mini-lists are on simple one-sided cards. Several owners have told me that to experiment, they have placed one or two better wines on their short lists and they sell well. In each case the wines are given bin numbers and carefully explained. Many believe that the popularity of half bottles is a sign of a beginning of better wine sales.

The After Dinner Menu   As the degree of interest in gourmet cooking has grown nationally, an interest in after-dinner desserts, cordials, and wines has also grown. Coffee is no longer plain coffee, it is Jamaican, Veronique, or Irish. Ice cream is now served with a cordial that brings out the flavor. Cream pies appear topped with the flavoring cordial that was used in baking.

The after-dinner dessert menu can be relatively simple. On one side are listed the special desserts, on the other, the list of dessert wines (Sauterne, Barsac, Asti, etc.) then a list of fine cordials

(Amaretto, Grand Marnier, Kahlúa, Drambuie, B & B, etc.). Last should be listed a range of cognacs and French brandies, by name and grade. This list is presented only upon the conclusion of the meal. With its exciting names and appetite-compelling descriptions, it is most difficult for the guest to turn down. The after-dinner menu can also be illustrated. One clever after-dinner list shows the chef leaving through one door and the server with a cordial cart coming through the other in New Yorker cartoon style. A second listing reproduces a picturesque English steel etching, showing the men with their port and cigars. The caption reads, "Where have the women gone?" The after-dinner market has been approached by modest-priced restaurants at a different level. At one restaurant, the table tent reads, on one side, "You don't have to be royalty to enjoy our Strawberries Romanoff." The illustration is a hard-hat worker enjoying dessert. The reverse carries the message, "And a glass of cordial doesn't take a king's ransom; name your flavor." The owner states that his single dessert specialty table tents have been so enthusiastically received that he is continuing the program. Another tactic that was employed by a budget-concerned establishment was: "Order our crepes suzette—and have a cordial on us."

Because so many diners don't leave room for dessert, it is clever merchandising to present dessert selections along with the dinner menu. In a Fort Worth, Texas, establishment, a mini book is stapled into the center of the menu. The book is titled, "Don't forget our 'Finishing Touch'—A Warning to Our Diners." The booklet then lists their fabulous desserts. Diners are warned that, should they overeat, they'll miss the delicacies. We live in a world where increasing numbers of people desire the better things in life. For instance, brioche and croissants, which used to be found in only limited fine dining places years ago, now appear in the supermarket freezer. Saying it all is the caption on an after-dinner dessert menu in Phoenix, "You count calories all week long. Here, count your blessings."

SELLING THE ROMANCE OF WINE

Wine listings can add to the adventure and romance of wine pleasure by supplying the customer with definitions. One such list gives the various phrases used in wine terminology, and explains the significance of over fifteen such as, "aged in the cask," and "generic." Another list defines label words: dolce—sweet, vendemmia—vintage. Both concepts serve to place the user on notice that this is a knowledgeable house of wine. To be willing to help without embarrassment creates customer goodwill.

As wine lists become increasingly broadened and wine users become increasingly knowledgeable, a specific indication of correct pronunciation for the server and the guest becomes essential—for example, Liebfraumilch, with a parenthesis alongside (leeb-frow milk), or Pouilly-Fuisse (Pooye-Phweseh). Even where the bin number is available and the wine name is used, phonetic spelling prevents misunderstanding. Valpolicella is a mouthful but "Val-pole-ee-chel-la" is simple. The degree to which lists go into depth, region, and history makes stress on enunciation more compatible and less frightening to the reader.

A major airline has produced a booklet titled "Cellar in the Sky." This booklet gives names and explanations of the wines that will be served on the flight. To remove the banality of endless blocks of type there are interesting line illustrations having to do with wine production, as well as a section called "Tips on Tasting." Were you the guest, would you prefer to reach for a list that stated "Wine List," "The Wines of Our House," "Carte des Vins," "From Our Cellars," "A Symphony in Wine, Libretto by (owner's name)," or "A Tour of Our Vineyards"?

Imagination will run rife when a wine list includes, for example, reproductions of Thomas Jefferson's letters that have to do with wine. This can break up the solemnity of a straightforward wine list. There are endless proverbs, sayings, and adages that can fit into the total wine list concept.

As the wine lover becomes more knowledgeable, he or she is more demanding in specifics. The use of simple maps will turn a blasé listing into a tour of the wine world. These maps can be simplified, broken into areas, and spaced to conform with wine categories. One such professional presentation is used by a major gourmet restaurant. The first four pages show maps of the best known wine-producing areas in California, broken down by county. Each map is numbered and relates to the number on the wine list.

Fig. 21 Wine list cover. Photo courtesy of Bohn-Bettoni Collection, University of Nevada, Las Vegas Library.

An ancient steel etching picturing wine being produced by "foot-treading" is reproduced on the cover for the wine list of a Spanish restaurant in Florida. To the restaurant with a larger budget, embossing will add dimension. A cask or cluster of grapes becomes alive and memorable with deep embossing. The secret is to emphasize the glamour and pleasure of wine without overwhelming the guest and the list.

Not every establishment will carry a superb wine selection. Yet to the customer, his or her wine order is an occasion that sets the meal apart from everyday living. Thus the presentation should be consistent with the pricing of the meal, the decor, and the clientele. The more moderate the dinner price, the greater the importance of wine.

As the use of wine has increased, the guest is often concerned about the kind of wine he is expected to order. Placing the recommended wine beneath the individual entrée assists the diner in his wine selection. The greater the degree of information given, the more interested the patron. To add authority, one eating place states: "Our Chef Recommends (name of wine)." Above the red meat entrées another place says, "Traditionally red wines are best enjoyed with red meats," and uses similar phrases on fowl, fish, and salads, urging the patron to better his meal with wine. The recommendation of a champagne, brandy, or cordial with desserts becomes a reminder to the patron to complete his dinner. Each memorandum encourages a sale that might be overlooked. While for many years only coffee was offered to end a meal, stimulating new coffee concepts have been introduced. Coffee Sambuca, Amaretto, Irish Coffee, Keoki, Coffee Veronica, and Jamaican Coffee lure the customer to new dessert drinks. Only through the statement on the menu will the order be given.

PRICING

On the wine list, prices must be clearly stated. The top of the column must be clear: full bottle, half bottle. With today's metric mix-up, even the sophisticated quaffer must be told the number of ounces. When the line reads "750 ml. (25.4 ounces)," the statement is unquestionable. The uninitiated appreciate definitions of full and half bottle content. The Appellation Controllée, QBA, or DOC can be documented on your menu. In presenting wines the category must be spelled out so that there remains little room for price discussion or error. Such phrases as "naturally fermented," "Château bottled," "Private label," "Riserva," when explained, point out the added worth of the bottle.

Although it is not the purpose of this work to discuss pricing in detail, it is worth mentioning that most hotels are undergoing a structure change from three times cost down to two and a half, while most restaurants are double costing. A problem of today's wine world is that the customer is making substantial purchases at wine stores and supermarkets. He or she is well aware of what prices are charged for national brands, and is able to quickly calculate mark-up. One severe article in a major newspaper castigated certain resort hotels for "ripping-off" customers on wine pricing. They were able to display the retail price of known wines which they compared with the price on the wine lists. The customer is not concerned with the cost of storage, maintenance, inventory control, and labor cost, unless these are explained. One expects the diner who orders a first growth to be aware of these factors, but such a customer may also try to display his or her knowledge by questioning price. The penalties of overcharging are severe, for in the mind of the customer the price of the wine reflects on the price being charged for food. The current practice of many large scale hotel and restaurant chains is to sell wine under either their own name or under the secondary labels of major shippers. As more new wine drinkers come on the scene it is best to explain through a brief statement that wine prices vary with demand.

SUMMARY

The competitive world of dining and wining will never leave well enough alone. This industry is one that creates a competitor and an idea each day. The price level of this industry is never as important as the image it projects with its printed literature. One of my first gourmet restaurants in the Fifty-ninth Street area of New York, was a French restaurant, and their menu cover was a colorful lithograph of Brittany. Inside was a lengthy list of specialties, handwritten in French. The word "Vins" on the cover of the wine list was the ultimate proof that I was dining as a Frenchman. Later, when I was in Paris, it was a source of great pleasure to me to enter the Deux Mâgots, Fouquets, and Les Lyonnaise, and discover the same style of presentation.

We are all affected by many issues that do not directly concern the wine and food. The wine list and menu represent the establishment. The look that has been designed, the care and concern for readability and contents directly affect the customer. If the printing is sloppy and blurred, the customer is embarrassed because pricing is difficult to read. If the cover is clever and arty, if the menu as a whole is responsive to the decor of the restaurant, and the wording is clear and informative, then the customer begins with great expectations.

Simplicity is majestic. If a menu is worth printing it is worth caring about. A neighborhood diner or local deli will spend no more by the use of white space and simple type than by the use of a mad hodgepodge of bold black with funereal trims. Compare a non-laminated menu to one that is laminated. There is a softness, a texture to the illustrations that is replaced by hard glare with the addition of the plastic. The treasurer's office will present the facts on how many printings are saved when lamination is used, but those figures do not show how many customers have the feeling of being mechanical eating robots.

I respect the pizza chain that displays above the counter each dish in a wonderfully soft transparency, attractively back lit. In the background of each photo is a scene of Italy. The planning and execution of these transparencies was worth every effort. Here is realistic appetite appeal with atmosphere.

We all enjoy having a menu and list that we have designed presented to the customer and receiving a mighty accolade, "Isn't that unusual? What a handsome presentation." At that point half the battle has been won. The customer assumes that the food and wine will be of matching calibre.

The ultimate creative aim of your wine list and menu is that it reflects in every way your establishment. Therefore in every phase they are worthy of your total creative effort, and your personal consideration.

APPENDIX

APPENDIX

All through history, wine has been a symbol of hospitality—and beginning with the Greeks who added honey, sweet wines have been favorites to serve guests. To make wine all you have to do is crush fresh, ripe grapes in a cup; the juice will turn to wine in time.

It happens partly as a result of that frosty bloom you see on the skin of the grape, which contains wild wine yeasts and the optimum amount of sugar to turn into a pleasing drink. No other fruit or berry on earth has these yeasts and the correct amount of sugar for spontaneous natural vintage. These wild wine yeasts just appear in the air, a different grouping in every vineyard. Somehow they sort themselves out every year, and around 100,000 of the right kind collect on the skin of each grape, waiting their chance to turn the sugar inside into alcohol.

Sun, wind, air temperature and humidity, the amount of rainfall, all these climatic conditions influence the character of wine. The wine expert knows local climatic variations. This depends on the "lie" of a vineyard, which direction it faces, the angle of incline, the intensity of the sun's reflection from a river, or perhaps, a protective mountain top. Every location has its special local climate, which gives the wine its own individual taste. Soil also plays a decisive role in the quality of the wine. A fine vine and a temperate climate do not guarantee good wine unless the soil is right. The vine sinks its roots deep into the earth and derives its mineral content from it.

What exactly happens during the elaborate process which takes the vine to the wineglass? In the late winter, the vines are pruned. The object is to skillfully rejuvenate and retain their growing strength. In the late spring the overgrown shoots are pruned, and the green ones cut back. The earth is then hoed, loosened, fertilized, and the weeds cleared.

Many additional measures are taken to protect the vine. It is defended against late frosts by covering, by smoke screens, or even by heating. But wine growers fear diseases and infestation even more than frost. It is necessary to constantly spray the vineyard. Today, special protective preparations prevent catastrophes which were devastating in the past. But there is no way of changing the weather. Too much rain is just as bad as too little. And the spring sunshine does hardly any good if the sun does not ripen the grapes in later summer and autumn. So the winegrower's success to a large extent is dependent upon natural causes.

From the time the grapes ripen until they are gathered, nothing and no one is allowed to disturb the vines as they grow. After this "autumn curfew" in the vineyards, harvest time comes and the first test for sugar content takes place. After the harvest, which occurs in early September for the early grapes and at the end of November for the late varieties, the grapes are crushed to a fruity pulp known as "mash." From the mash the sugar content ("must") is pressed out and the cloudy, still unfermented juices of the grapes are extracted. The fresh juice is immediately drawn off into barrels (these days more often into tanks), and after a few days it begins to ferment.

Microscopically small organisms—the wine yeast in the grapes —now become very lively and multiply the moment they come into contact with the glucose in the juice, splitting the glucose into carbonic acid and alcohol. The carbonic acid escapes as it develops through the bung hole at the top of the barrel which functions as an air vent. After several weeks, the fermentation process is complete. The glucose in the grapes has turned into carbonic acid and alcohol, completely if the fruit contained little sugar, or partially in the case of very sweet grapes. If the wine has reached an alcohol content of 12 to 14 percent, the fermentation stops automatically even if the yeast finds still more glucose to split up. The strength of the alcohol content, which the wine yeast has produced, kills the yeast, which sinks to the bottom of the barrel as sediment.

Fermentation also creates considerable heat, and cooling devices are used to keep the temperature down. These are often installed right in the fermenting vats. If the yeasts are permitted to convert all the sugar, the resulting wine is "dry." When some sweetness is wanted, the fermentation is stopped while the proper proportion of grape sugar remains. To produce a non-dry table wine (such as sweet Sauterne) the fermentation is halted by the addition of a small quantity of sulphur dioxide or by pasteurization. In the making of a dessert wine, fermentation is stopped by the addition of brandy at the proper time; the sweetness is sometimes increased by the addition of grape concentrate.

Color in the wine usually comes from the grape skins. So, in order to produce a red wine, fermentation proceeds with the skins left in the vat. To make a pink or rosé wine, the skins are permitted to remain in the fermenting wine for only a short period until a little color has been drawn out of the skins, and then the juice is siphoned off the skins and is permitted to ferment alone. A white wine is produced simply by fermentation of the juice alone right from the start.

When the fermentation is completed, the new wine goes into storage casks to begin the process of aging, which may take months or years, depending on the type and quality of the wine. In storage, some of the grape solids in the wine settle or deposit to the sides and bottom of the casks. These deposits are called "lees" the settling is heaviest in young wines, but continues in the oldest as well (which is why some wine bottles show a crust or film of sediment after varying periods of age).

After proper aging, the wines are often blended. This is an art based on experience. Some grapes produce wines with a number of desirable characteristics but lacking in others. By blending, all the required elements can be properly proportioned in the wine that is to be bottled. Before bottling, the wine is made brilliantly clear. This is called "finishing" the wine, and is done by sending the wine through filters, by storing it in cold rooms for varying periods of time, or sometimes by letting clarifying substances settle through the wine. This last method is called "fining," and involves adding some gelatinous material (isinglass, white of egg, etc.) which drops slowly through the wine, carrying with it the suspended particles in the wine. The wine is then ready for the bottling line and for the market, though many vintners bin their wines to achieve some "bottle aging" before sending it into trade channels.

GENERAL WINE CLASSIFICATIONS

Table wine is the general classification for those wines which are consumed with the main courses of luncheon or dinner. They are usually dry to medium sweet in taste, and have an alcoholic content of twelve percent. Table wines are also classified by color: red, white, and rosé. The color of the wine does not necessarily reflect the color of the grapes used in making it, but rather happens as a step in the production.

BORDEAUX—RED　　All red bordeaux wines are produced from varieties of the Cabernet vine and are, in almost all cases, blends of various authorized varieties developed by the growers as best representative of the district in which they were grown and from which they take their name. Bordeaux is the land of the famed châteaux from which the greatest names in wine are shipped.

BURGUNDY—RED　　Burgundy, in French *Bourgogne*, is a province southeast of Paris which produces less than two percent of French wines. Included in that small amount, however, are some of the best known wines of the world with its reds on par with those of the châteaux of Bordeaux. Grapes most used for these reds are the Pinot Noir and the Gamay, both of which also do well in the United States, where the varietal wines from these grapes hold their own with the best Burgundy has to offer. Beaujolais wines, produced in the southern part of Burgundy, are now known primarily by their

own names although the reds are true burgundies. Bottles follow the
Burgundy tradition with long sloping shoulders.

CONCORD—RED   The Concord is a blue-black American
grape bred early in the nineteenth century from native American
grapes which included the Catawba, the grape used for much of the
wines made in the East, in the Finger Lake and Hammondsport
areas. Concord is the basis for all unfermented grape juice and for
most of the grape jelly made in the United States. As a wine, it is
heavily sugared and not normally suitable with meals.

ITALIAN WINES—RED   Piedmont, "foot of the mountain," is
the extreme northwest corner of Italy. This region produces two of
Italy's finest red wines, Barolo and Barbaresco, both from the Heb-
bido grape, and a number of minor wines named for other grapes
from the region. These wines have their counterparts in major
United States production. DOC, for *Denominazione di Origine
Controllata*, is the Italian equivalent of the French Government
designation of A.C. *Appellation Controllée*, and indicates that wines
so labeled have achieved stipulated standards for quality.

WHITE WINES   These wines are produced from white grapes,
black grapes, or a combination of both. Grapes are pressed, however, rather than squeezed as for red wines, and skins are not
permitted to add color to the wine. The result is a taste of freshness
which is enhanced by the cold temperature at which these wines
should be served. In the United States, any white table wine,
wherever made and of whatever grapes, may call itself chablis. True
counterparts to the varietal imports will be found in the Pinot
Chardonnay group.

BORDEAUX—WHITE   White is really the wrong word for
wines in this category. Any wine which is not distinctly red or pink is
described as white, whether it is really the palest possible gold or
almost brown. Although there is a much greater variety of white
wines than red, Bordeaux produces only two major types, graves, a
dry to medium sweet table wine and sauternes, a sweet dessert

wine. Both are made from the Semillon and Sauvignon Blanc grapes which are also responsible for the high quality of the best California white wines.

BURGUNDY—WHITE   Less than a quarter of the wines made in Burgundy are white, but, experts say, the best white still table wines are included in this production, surpassing even those of Bordeaux where sweetness takes wines such as sauternes out of the table class into after-dinner usage. Burgundy whites are all of the dry type, low in sweetness, and the best are all produced from the Chardonnay grape with some blending from the Pinot Blanc.

LOIRE WINES—WHITE   Loire, a region north of Bordeaux, stretches the length of the Loire River and produces a great variety of wines. Few Loires are well known outside of Europe except the rosés as they are not long-lived and are best drunk young. Recently, some of the better types have been exported. In the whites, the vouvray, with its dry-sweet characteristics, won many converts when VDQS (*Vin Delimite de Qualité Superieure*), in World War I, was set up in Tours. Muscadet has become a well-known import, as well. Chenin Blanc is the grape used in vouvray and in most of the better Loire wines.

PORTUGUESE WINES—WHITE   *Vinho Verde* (Green Wines) of Portugal are not what they seem in that the name means young and sprightly, not immature. They are refreshing warm weather drinks, light in alcohol, and only recently have become available for export.

RHINE/MOSELLE—WHITE   Although wines of the French Rhineland are not called Rhine wines due to rulings made before World War I when Germany controlled Alsace, they are produced from the same grapes as those grown in the German Rhineland and have many of the same characteristics. The better Alsatian wines, unlike those from the rest of France, carry the name of the grape, rather than the place of origin, under government controls. Germany has the distinction of being able to produce fine wines in the coldest and least friendly climate for vines of any other important

zone. Almost all are white, primarily from the Riesling grape, or its varieties, and come from areas in the Rhineland or from the valley of the River Moselle.

ROSÉ WINES   Rosé, a more dignified word for pink, is the universal wine, produced in all wine-making countries and useful for almost all occasions. Despite its similarity of color, it comes in a great variety of tastes, mostly contrived by the makers to suit the greatest number of devotees they can attract. It is made entirely from black grapes with skins left in the juice only for a short time and removed before the wine loses the special tint for which it is known. Grapes used are primarily the Grenache and the Gamay, with native vines responsible for the popular Portuguese rosés.

"POP" WINES   "Pop" wine is a recent phenomenon in the wine industry where it has built an enormous popularity due to a general desire for lighter beverages. The younger generation has indicated its preference for the unassuming wines included in this category over higher strength alcoholic drinks and, despite dire predictions from the conservative experts, the preference seems to be here to stay.

APERITIF AND DESSERT WINES   Most dessert wines have a relatively high sugar content, but these wines also have their dry types as well as all of the variations between sweet and dry. Aperitif and dessert wines are raised to twenty percent alcoholic content by the addition of brandy during the fermentation process. This has the effect of stopping fermentation of the wine sugar. The timing of the brandy dosage establishes the degree of sweetness, or dryness, of the finished product.

APERITIFS—VERMOUTHS   Vermouth comes from the German *Wermut*, wormwood, a shrub whose flowers produce the aromatic agent found in this fortified wine. (A wine is "fortified" when brandy is added for greater strength and alcoholic content.) Used as an aperitif and as a cocktail ingredient, vermouth is produced in two main types: French, or dry, and Italian, or sweet.
     Proprietary, or patent aperitifs are greatly similar to vermouths

when taken before meals as appetizers in that they are usually of higher proof and always contain secret ingredients as sources of their distinctive taste. All originate in foreign countries, where their popularity is much greater than in the United States. Other aperitifs include champagne, dry sherry, madeira and port, wines which most experts believe to be best drunk before meals rather than with them.

CHAMPAGNE—WHITE

Still white wines are made sparkling by the addition of sugar and yeast to stimulate fermentation in the bottle. The designation of dryness, when shown on the label, indicates how much sugar and wine syrup was added when sediment from fermentation was removed, or "disgorged," from the bottle: Brut, dosage of up to 1½ percent; Extra Dry, up to three percent; Dry or Sec, up to four percent or more. The low priced American champagnes are made possible by a process developed in 1910 by the French wine scientist, Eugene Charmat. Still wines are fermented in bulk in large tanks to produce a continuous flow of sparkling wine of sound but uninspiring quality.

CHAMPAGNE—ROSÉ (PINK)

Champagne owes a great deal of its flavor and bouquet to the fact that it is usually blended from wines produced from both white, Pinot Chardonnay, and black, Pinot Noir, grapes. The color is not affected by the black grapes as skins are removed from the juice before fermentation. However, if fermentation is allowed for two or three days before removing the skins, enough color is added to give the final blend the attractive cast of pink champagne, a feature of many memorable parties. In serving, or being served champagne, avoid at all costs the saucer-on-a-stem better suited for sherbets. Almost any other type of glass will preserve the bubbles and it is the bubbles which make champagne. Following is a list of champagne types:

Brut—relatively dry, and hence an appropriate companion to the widest variety of foods.

Extra Dry—a medium dry champagne for those who prefer a hint of sweetness. A very pleasant and enjoyable companion at parties, during meals, and with desserts.

Sec—by nature slightly sweet with a gentle and refreshing character. A superb choice with desserts and after dining.

Rosé—a delightful pink champagne, the perfect blend of select champagne grapes, including Pinot Noir and Pinot Chardonnay. The light, dry taste makes it a truly versatile companion with all foods, and its delicate pink color adds a festive touch to any occasion.

SPARKLING WINES   Champagne processes are used in the making of a number of other sparkling wines, all of which have enthusiastic followers. Best known is the sparkling burgundy, made from a variety of grapes and mostly on the sweet side. Then there are the crackling rosés, carbonated or naturally sparkling in a light way suitable for dining accompaniment. Newcomers are the cold ducks, fabulously popular blends of sparkling wines which have the taste and appearance of a mixture of equal parts of champagne and sparkling burgundy.

The history of cold duck is shrouded in mystery and antiquity. Centuries ago, it was the custom in Germany to combine the wines which were left at the end of the evening meal. These combined wines were then chilled. This concoction was known as *kaltes ende* (German translation—cold ending). Over the years, either from a printer's negligence or by an imaginative punster, *kaltes ende* became *kalte ente* which literally translated into English means cold duck. This name has been adopted by Americans to refer to a mixture of white and red champagnes.

AMERICAN WINES

In 1518, Cortez introduced wine making as an industry to the Western Hemisphere, starting on a very small scale in Mexico. Nearly two centuries later, William Penn and others tried to cultivate European grapes for wine in the eastern section of the United

States, but all their attempts met with complete failure. Before this time, however, early settlers in this area had discovered wild grapes, and these grape strains eventually became the foundation of a wine industry which still flourishes in New York state and Ohio. The wines produced from the eastern United States grapes are different in character and flavor from those made in California, where vineyards have been cultivated from the European grape species. The major varieties of grapes were introduced from Europe in the early nineteenth century and later, following a disastrous vine disease in Europe, cuttings from the American grapes were taken back to help restart the European wine industry. As time passed many hybrid grapes were developed to specially match the soil and conditions of the United States.

Commercial wine making in California actually began in 1825 when Joseph Chapman planted 4,000 vines near Los Angeles. But the true birth of the California wine industry occurred in 1848 when California joined the United States and the Gold Rush began. These events created a demand for the wines of the young industry. The hilly sections north, east, and south of San Francisco Bay have a cool climate with sufficient rain to make artificial irrigation unnecessary for vineyards. Most of the grapes grown in this section produce superior table wines. California's fertile central valley has a rather hot, dry climate, similar to that of Spain and Portugal. Practically all the grapes for dessert wines such as ports, sherries and muscatels, are grown in the middle section of this valley. To the southeast of Los Angeles lies the so-called Cucamonga district. Grapes grown in this area produce both table wines and dessert wines. California's climate is considered to be one of the best in the world for growing fine wine grapes. The even rainfall and clear sunny days provide such excellent growing conditions that vintage indications are unnecessary. Every year is a vintage year in California.

In recent years, an important change has been taking place in the wine business. The market for premium wines, high-quality table wines, and dessert wines has been booming as more and more people become aware of the excellent quality of American wines. Although other states have tried growing the Vitis Vinifera grapes, only the climate and soils of California have proven suitable for it.

This is the true wine grape species from which all European and California wines are made.

Generic wines are those named for their place of origin. American generic wines may have a name reflecting the European area where similar type wines originated. The name "Burgundy," for instance, is descriptive of a wine similar in character to those made in the French Burgundy district. In order to properly inform the consumer, American label regulations stipulate that the generic name must be preceded by the word "California" when made in that state. Example: "California Burgundy." A varietal wine is named for the grape used in making it. Varietal wines are not as such better than generic wines. The choice of a wine is always determined by personal taste preference.

The information on the labels of all bottles of American wines is regulated by Federal law. In addition, California has its own set of laws governing the labeling of California wines. In most instances, the California law is stricter, and supersedes the Federal regulations. Some of the rules regarding labeling of bottles are as follows:

1. Estate bottled. This means that you grow your grapes exclusively in your own vineyards and bottle your own wine at your own winery. It is the strictest wine regulation in the United States.
2. Vintage. The year in which the wine was made. It's a guarantee of a wine's maturity.
3. Varietal. The United States Government states that to carry this term on the label, at least fifty-one percent of the wine must come from a particular variety of grape.
4. District. By law, seventy-five percent of the grapes must come from a certain grape-growing district before the name of the district can be printed on the label.
5. Produced and bottled. If a wine label says bottled by, the wine can be from any place. Even if it says made and bottled by, this means that only ten percent of the wine must be from that winery. Produced and bottled by means that the entire winemaking process takes place on the premises.

TYPICAL FRENCH WINES

BORDEAUX

Bordeaux Rouge (Red): This moderately priced wine is a blend of grapes gathered in the Bordeaux region and has the delicacy and charm common to Bordeaux wines.

Médoc: Some of the famous parishes of Médoc are St. Estephe, Pauillac, St. Julien, Moulis, and Margaux. The wines of Medoc are red. They are light bodied and unique in the world for their elegant fragrance, their mellowness, and their delicate, long lasting taste.

St. Emilion: The wines of this region are red, full-bodied, robust. They have a strong bouquet and a distinguished taste.

Pomerol: A very small district. Its wines are red, a little lighter than the St. Emilion with which they share most of the characteristics of bouquet and taste.

Graves: Graves produces both red and white wines. The whites may be either dry or medium dry. They are well balanced, elegant wines with a delicate bouquet and a fruity flavor.

Sauternes: Sauternes, which includes the township of Barsac, produces the greatest naturally sweet wines in the world. They have a beautiful deep golden color. They are mellow, very fruity, with a long lasting, rich flavor.

Bottled Bordeaux are of two principal types: regional bottlings and château bottlings. Meaning literally castle, château is the Bordeaux term for vineyard estate, some of which sport real castles and some of which do not. A château bottled wine is one which will have been bottled at the vineyard where the grapes were grown and the wine will therefore have come from that specific place.

Regional and parish bottlings also come from a specific place, but now the place is the district or *Appellation d'Origine Controlée,* rather than an individual vineyard. Château wines stand or fall with the reputation of the vineyard owner; regional bottlings are guaranteed by the reputation of the shipper.

BURGUNDY   The wines of Burgundy have warmth and a strong bouquet. They are full-bodied and mellow. The whites are very dry. Burgundy wines are sold under the name of the township or district they come from. Those bottled in the same estate where they are made and aged bear the name of that estate with one of the following sentences on the label: *"Mise de la Propriété"; "Mise en Bouteille par le Propriétaire"; "Mise du Domaine"; "Mise en Bouteille au Domaine."* The region of Burgundy may be divided into:

Chablis. The small town of Chablis north of Burgundy produces a dry, white wine so famous that it has been imitated in many other countries. The wine of Chablis is very dry, light, and heady. It has a characteristic flavor, usually described as flinty. Its color is a light yellow with a slightly greenish overtone.

The Côte d'Or. This area, which produces the greatest of the great Burgundies, is divided into two parts: The Côte de Nuits to the north and the Côte de Beaune to the south.

a. Côte de Nuits—the wines of the Côte de Nuits are very full-bodied and generous, with a remarkable bouquet. The best known come from the following townships: Fixin, Gevreychambertin, Morey-Saint-Denis, Chambolle-Musigny, Vougeot, Flagey-Echezeaux, Vosne-Romanée, and Nuits-Saint-Georges.
b. Côte be Beaune—The wines of Côte de Beaune are somewhat lighter than those of Côte de Nuits. They are delicate and smooth with a very strong bouquet. The whites are dry and fruity and rank among the very best.

The principal townships are: Aloxe-Corton, Pernand-Vergelesses, Beaune, Pommard, Volnay, Meursault, Chassagne and Puligny-Montrachet.

SOUTHERN BURGUNDY   The wines of southern Burgundy
are lighter than the Côte d'Or wines. They are fruity with a delicate
bouquet. They have freshness and are excellent when young. Southern Burgundy includes the regions of Chalon, Macon and Beaujolais. Chalon produces the well known wines of Mercurey, Rully,
Gevrey, and Montagny. Macon Blanc is made from the superb Pinot
Chardonnay grape and is rapidly becoming an American favorite. It
is a dry, full flavored wine of much charm. The wines of Beaujolais
are fresh, light with an earthy flavor and bouquet. They are best
when young. The principal wines of Beaujolais are: Saint-Amour,
Julienas, Fleurie, Chiroubles, Morgon, Côte De Brouilly, and
Moulin-à-Vent.

CHAMPAGNE   The wine of Champagne is one of the most fa-
mous of all French wines. Since it was invented by a monk, Dom
Perignon, at the end of the seventeenth century, it has been associated everywhere with festivities and celebrations. However, it is also
an excellent dinner wine and goes well with almost any dish. By
French law, wines may be called Champagne only if they are made
from grapes grown in the Champagne region.

Champagne is always a blend. Grapes from different vineyards
are pressed separately and blended in the *cuvé*. Each great champagne firm has its own standard in blending, and the reputation of
the champagne producer is the best guarantee of quality. Non-
vintage wines from a reputable firm often equal or even surpass a
vintage wine from an obscure house.

ALSACE   The region of Alsace which spreads along the French
bank of the Rhine produces dry, fresh, fruity, white wines. Although
the wines of this region, alone among French wines, are sold under
the grape variety name, the label must also read "Appellation Controlée Alsace." The principal wines of Alsace are:

Riesling—a very dry, elegant and classic wine.

Gewurztraminer—a very fruity, supple wine which holds the dis-
tinction of having probably the greatest bouquet of any wine in the
world.

Traminer—of the same family as the Gewurztraminer but lighter in bouquet and flavor.

Sylvaner—a fresh, light, fruity wine.

Alsatian wines are served chilled. They make delightful aperitifs and may be served throughout the meal.

CÔTES DU RHONE   The red wines of Côte du Rhone are full-bodied with vigor and warmth. They have a rich bouquet and a luscious taste. Within Côtes du Rhone, other principal wines come from: Côte-Rotie, Saint-Peray, Lirac, Tavel, and Chateauneuf-du-Pape.

THE LOIRE   Delightful wines are produced along the lovely banks of the Loire River. Those wines, whether red, rosé, or white, are fresh, light, and delicately fruity.

The best known are: the dry, still white wines of Pouilly-Fumé and Sancerre; the still and crackling white wines of Vouvray which range from dry to sweet; the red wines of Chinon and Bourgueil; and the white wines (dry or sweet) of Saumur Anjou, which produces about half of the wines of the Loire. These are red, white, and rosé. However, half of this area's production is its popular rosé which is a slightly sweet, soft, and mellow wine.

The wines of the Loire are drunk when they are young. The whites and rosés are chilled. The reds lose none of their charm by being cooled.

E.E.C. LEGISLATION   Most wine-growing areas in the world have legislation which controls the amount and quality of wine production in each district. As far as E.E.C. (European Economic Community) countries are concerned, the best known legislation is the French system of Appellation Controlée (the Germans and the Italians also have laws based on very much the same lines).

When, in 1934, legislation was introduced to provide a fair deal for the wine grower in France, the market was very different from that of today. In those days wine was very inexpensive. Growers found it difficult to make a living. So this Wine Code, generally referred to as the legislation of Appellation Controlée, covered three main points:

1. The control of the naming of individual vineyards, parishes, districts, or areas of production. (Different types of soil vary in suitability for producing wines, and these areas had to be defined.)

2. The maximum quantity they could produce per hectare (approx. 2½ acres) of vineyard to enable the wines to carry the names of these vineyards, parishes, or areas. (As a general rule, the more wine an acre of vines produces, the lower the quality of the wine is likely to be. But with greatly improved methods, these maximum quantities as originally laid down now seem quite outdated.)

3. The level of alcohol in each wine in order for it to carry the name of the vineyard, parish, or area. (Alcohol is important for the character, stability and length of life of the wine.)

It is no secret that many French vineyards, particularly in a good year, produce more than their official maximum yield as laid down by the laws of Appellation Controlée. But this surplus is not entitled to be bottled and labeled as Appellation Controlée although the wine is the same as that which receives the Appellation entitlement.

Hitherto, the wine merchant has been able to buy, for example, Nuits-St. Georges that was surplus to the Appellation Controlée entitlement. The French shipper would sell this surplus Nuits-St. Georges at a lower price than the same wine with the Appellation certificate.

And so customers have come to enjoy Nuits-St. Georges (and a lot of other wines too), which has cost less than the same wine sold in France.

Take an example of how this has worked:

A vineyard in the Burgundy District

Official maximum yield	= 100 casks
Actual yield	= 130 casks

Price of 100 casks with A.C. Certificates is 100 units ea.
Price of 30 casks of the same quality wine without A.C.
Certificates is 60 units ea.

This simply means that your favorite wines may in the future be called by the wine merchant's own name, instead of the vineyard name to which you have grown accustomed.

TYPICAL GERMAN WINES

RIESLING   (White) This is the finest and best known of the white wines grown in Germany. Its especially small grapes ripen late, in November or even December. Despite a lengthy ripening time, during which the grapes accumulate a great deal of glucose, Riesling does not taste too sweet, but remains richly piquant and vivacious, with a fruity taste.

SYLVANER   (White) Sylvaner vines, like Riesling, are cultivated over a quarter of the German wine area. Its fruit is bigger and ripens earlier. Also, yields are higher than Riesling. Typical Sylvaner tastes mild and fruity.

SPATBURGUNDER   (Red) Like Riesling among the white wines, Spatsburgunder is undisputed as the finest variety of German red wine. Originally from the old French province of Burgundy, it later became indigenous to Germany. Typical Spatburgunder is velvety and fruity.

TROLLINGER   (Red) This wine is light with an especially fresh taste. The vine was taken to Württemberg from its original home in the Tirol.

PORTUGIESER   A red wine in no way associated with Portugal, this wine comes from the Rhenish Palatinate and Hesse. More of it is drunk in Germany than any other German red wine, where it is enjoyed as a good table wine.

The German wine laws have now been in effect for several years, resulting in several changes to names. Basically, the vineyards have been redesignated and gradings are awarded to wines, in respect to their quality, by a government panel of specialists.

Thus Niersteiner Domtal, Bernkasteler Riesling, and so on disappear, and become "Bereich," the German word meaning "the district of," e.g. Bereich Nierstein, Bereich Bernkastel.

The three gradings are as follows: (1) *Deutscher Tafelwein* (German Table Wine)—a wine not from any specific area. (2) *Qualitatswein* (Quality Wine)—Wine from a specific area (e.g. Bereich Nierstein) having passed tests for quality. All Liebfraumilch must now fall into this category, and all these wines must be bottled in the vicinity. (3) *Qualitatswein mit Pradikat* (Quality wine of special merit)—all Spatlese and Auslese wines fall into this category. These will almost always be single vineyard wines and they will have passed even more stringent tests. All these must be either estate or locally bottled.

Five grades of highest quality, specially graded wines are allowed and mentioned on the label.

Kabinett An elegant, fully ripened wine, harvested at the normal time. Normal in Germany as a rule means October, a time when the grapes have long been gathered in the rest of Europe. It is this lengthy, slow ripening time which increases German wine's unique characteristics.

Spatlese These wines come from grapes harvested after the normal picking period. They are distinguished by a special elegance and ripeness and are appealingly round and delicious.

Auslese Produced from the fully ripened grapes which are specially sorted from the rest and pressed separately. Auslese wines reveal their elegance through their ripeness and full bouquet, and are unquestionably ideal for a special occasion.

Beerenauslese Represent a further increase in quality where the wine is made from ripe and over-ripe berries separated by hand. This results in a wonderful, mature, fruity, and full wine which possesses an unmistakable flowery aroma and a color like amber.

Trockenbeerenauslese This is wine of the very finest quality. Only grapes shriveled like raisins are pressed, offering significant characteristics in appearance and taste.

GLOSSARY

WINE TYPES

AUSLESE: German term signifying that a wine has been made from selected bunches of grapes.

BARBERA: A red wine grape which originated in the Piedmont district of Italy; also a heavy-bodied red table wine made from Barbera grapes.

BARSAC: A rather sweet white wine of pronounced bouquet.

BEERENAUSLESE: Made from individually selected berries of selected bunches.

BERNKASTEL: A noted winemaking district of the Moselle, Germany, celebrated for its "Doktor" wines.

BURGUNDY: A red table wine, heavier in body, darker in color than claret.

CABERNET: A red dry table wine in which the Cabernet Sauvignon grape predominates.

CHABLIS: A white table wine; dry, fruity, straw colored. A white burgundy.

CHAMPAGNE: White wine made effervescent by a second fermentation in a closed container. This produces gas (CO_2) which is trapped in the wine and escapes slowly when the bottle is opened, providing a sparkle to the wine. The colder the wine the slower the bubbles escape.

CHARDONNAY: A white grape that produces fine white table wines. Also called Pinot Chardonnay. One of the important grapes in the production of champagne.

CHIANTI: Dry, medium-bodied, ruby red, strongly flavored wine. Italian in character. Often, chianti is bottled in wicker-covered, bulbous flasks. White chianti is also produced, but to a lesser extent.

CLARET: A light, dry red table wine originally, the British name given to the red wines of Bordeaux, France.

CLEVENER: Red wine grape grown in New Jersey and the Finger Lakes wine region of New York state.

CONCORD: The most widely planted native American grape in the United States. Used in the production of the popular kosher type wines.

CUVÉ: Blend of still wines used in making champagne and other sparkling wines.

DELAWARE: Native American white wine grape.

FINO: A term applied to lightish-colored, fairly dry sherry.

FLAVORED WINES: Wines with various flavors added (citrus, coca, etc.). These have been gaining in popularity in the United States. Though classed as aperitif wines, many are sweet enough to be used for after-dinner drinks. Most such wines have been given forceful brand names.

FRANKEN RIESLING: White wine grape, and wines made from this grape. Also known as Sylvaner.

GAMAY: A grape used in the production of red wine. A sparse producer. The wine is sometimes sold under its varietal name (often gamay beaujolais), though more often blended into a Burgundy.

GEWURZTRAMINER: A grape and a wine named for the grape. The wine is marked by a spiciness that many find pleasant.

GRAVES: One of the districts in the Bordeaux area of France. Also a white table wine from that district.

GRENACHE: A wine grape which has won wide acceptance in the light rosé wines which are often produced from it. Also used in making port wine in California.

GREY RIESLING: A white wine grape, also a wine made from this grape.

HAUTE SAUTERNE: A white table wine sweeter than ordinary sauterne.

HOCKE: A term used (mainly in England but sometimes in the United States) for dry white table wines of the Rhine type.

JOHANNISBERG(ER) RIESLING: Some call it white Riesling. A very highly regarded white wine grape; also the name of the wine made from this grape.

LIEBFRAUMILCH: A white wine type from Germany's Rhine valley. Generally soft and slightly on the sweet side. Can vary widely in quality.

MADEIRA: An island off the west coast of Africa, noted for its trade in wines of this name. These are dark amber, of twenty percent alcohol, with a baked taste, and generally sweet.

MARSALA: A dark amber wine sweeter than sherry and Madeira.

MEDOC: The most important district in the Bordeaux region of France. Produces only clarets.

MOSELLE: A white wine made from grapes grown in the wine districts along the Moselle River in Germany. In California production, a light white wine of similar type.

NORTON: The best of the native American red wine grapes.

OLOROSO: A popular type of sherry, darker and somewhat sweeter than the Fino and Amontillado types.

PIEDMONT: An important province in northern Italy noted for its fine Barolo wines. It includes the Asti district.

PINOT BLANC: French white wine grapes. Also, a wine made predominantly from this grape.

PINOT NOIR: Choice red wine grape, used for making fine Burgundy.

PORT: Rich, heavy-bodied, sweet dessert wine of a tawny or ruby color.

RIESLING: A thoroughly dry, tart, white wine, with a slightly greenish-amber cast of color. Present wine nomenclature also refers to wines of this general type as California hock, California Rhine wine, or as California Moselle. These wines vary according to brands. A different wine is Johannisberg Riesling, which is of the same general type as California Riesling but which is made of the Johannisberg Riesling grape and has the flavor and aroma of that grape.

SAUTERNE: White table wine, dry, or slightly sweet, golden in color. In France, this wine type is always on the sweetish side. Only in the United States is there such a wine as a dry sauterne.

SAUVIGNON BLANC: White sauterne grape variety. Also a wine made from this grape.

SEC: A French word meaning dry. Used in the United States almost exclusively to describe champagnes—and strangely enough, signifies semi-sweet rather than dry.

SEMILLON: An important white wine grape used in choice sauternes. Also a wine made from this grape.

SHERRY: Appetizer wine with a nutty flavor, light to dark amber in color, ranges from dry to very sweet. Sherry is produced by use of a special yeast or by baking. Baking is done in specially heated vats, in heated rooms, or in some cases by placing the barrels in the open where the sun does the job.

SPUMANTE: Italian term for sparkling wine.

SYLVANER: White wine grape and wine produced from this grape. Also known as Franken Riesling.

TOKAY: A pink-colored sweet dessert wine of California, with a slightly nutty flavor, less sweet than port; distinct from the Tokay wine of Hungary.

TRAMINER: Choice white wine grapes. Also the name of a wine made from this grape.

VERMOUTH: Wine flavored with herbs and other aromatic substances. These are two types, French (dry, pale amber) and Italian (sweet, dark amber). The United States has developed a very light dry vermouth for use as a mixer. This is generally labeled extra dry or some similar term.

VIN ORDINAIRE: French term meaning good, sound, inexpensive wine.

VINO ROSSO: Italian for red wine. Used in the United States to describe the increasingly popular red wine from which the edge of dryness has been removed, sometimes by the addition of a slight amount of port. A mellow red table wine.

ZINFANDEL: A very widely planted red wine grape in California; also the name of wine made from this grape.

WINE TERMS

AGING: Maturing of the wine. The aging of the wine is at first very active in casks in the producer's cellars. It continues at a much slower pace in the bottle. Properly controlled aging makes the wine mellow and supple. Excessive aging results in the passing out of the wine. Only greater wines may gain by aging for decades. Most other wines are at their best when young, from one to five years, depending on the region of origin and the conditions of the vintage.

BRUT: Maximum of dryness.

CHILL: To cool the wine prior to serving it. This is done by letting the bottle stand for one hour in the refrigerator or about twenty-five minutes in an ice bucket. Too low a temperature is not advisable because it would freeze the aroma and flavor of the wine.

NON-VINTAGE WINES: Wines blended from several vintages in order to obtain a high standard of quality. Only non-vintage wines can be the same in quality from year to year.

ROOM TEMPERATURE: The temperature at which red wines are usually served, between 60° and 65°F.

SEDIMENT: Deposit which results from aging in the bottle. Sediment does not harm the wine in any way. It is very often an indication that the wine is a greater and older one. A bottle of wine showing sediment should be left to rest upright until the sediment has dropped to the bottom of the bottle. It should then either be decanted or poured carefully in order to allow only clear wine to pass into the glass.

WINE TASTING TERMS

One of the enduring joys of wine for many people is talking about the wines they are enjoying. This list of common wine tasting terms will help you and your guests to do that, in the accepted language of wine.

ACIDITY: The quality of tartness or sharpness in a wine—not to be confused with sourness, dryness, or astringency. The presence of agreeable fruit acids.

AROMA: That part of wine's fragrance originating from the grapes.

ASTRINGENCY: The puckeriness of wines, usually derived from tannin from the skins and seeds. Moderate astringency is considered desirable in most red table wines.

BALANCE: A pleasing proportion of sugar, acid, and other constituents of wine.

BODY: Consistency, thickness, or substance of wine, as opposed to lack of body in a thin wine.

BOUQUET: The part of wine's fragrance which originates from fermentation and aging, as distinguished from aroma.

CLEAR: No suspended solids in the wine, no cloudiness. A brilliant wine.

DRY: The absence of sweetness. Not to be confused with sour.

FRUITY: Having the fragrance and flavor of the grape, a freshness, sometimes called grapey.

MATURE: A wine that has developed all of its characteristic qualities.

MELLOW: A soft wine, often with some sweetness. Usually used in reference to some red table wines.

NOSE: Term for the total fragrance, aroma, and bouquet of a wine.

NUTTY: The characteristic pungent flavor of sherry.

ROUGH: A hard wine, immature, not well-balanced, or too astringent.

SOUND: A wine which is pleasant to look at, good smelling and tasting.

TART: Possessing agreeable acidity (as a touch of lemon makes food tart).